JN336351

英語長文
PREMIUM 問題集
Standard

▶ Standard　標　準 レベル
　 Advanced　上　級 レベル
　 Top　　　 最上級 レベル

☐ Lesson 01
☐ Lesson 02
☐ Lesson 03
☐ Lesson 04
☐ Lesson 05
☐ Lesson 06
☐ Lesson 07
☐ Lesson 08
☐ Lesson 09
☐ Lesson 10
☐ Lesson 11
☐ Lesson 12
☐ Lesson 13
☐ Lesson 14
☐ Lesson 15
☐ Lesson 16
☐ Lesson 17
☐ Lesson 18
☐ Lesson 19
☐ Lesson 20

【総合監修】
安河内哲也
Tetsuya Yasukochi

東進ハイスクール・東進衛星予備校 編

東進ブックス

まえがき
PREFACE

　本書は，大学入試における英語長文の読解力をしっかりと伸ばし，新たな「4技能試験」にも通じる「リーディング」の力も高めたいという人のために作られた，新しい英語長文問題集の決定版です。特に，最新の大学入試問題から適切な学習素材を選び，それを英検・TOEFL・TEAPなどの「4技能試験」に対応させながら学びやすくすることに力を入れて作られています。本書では，日本の大学入試問題の良問を厳選して3つのレベルに分割し，さらにそれを国際標準である「CEFR」という指標にも対応して配列することを目指しています。このことによって，あらゆる試験に対応した段階的な学習ができるようになっています。

　アイテム（問題文）の選択においては，多くの東進講師陣の力を結集し，膨大な入試問題データベースの中から最良の英文を厳選しました。語彙レベルや内容を徹底的に精査し，現在の大学入試だけでなく，4技能試験のリーディング対策としても使用できるものを抽出し，最終的に3レベル20題ずつ（合計60題）に絞り込みました。

　また，問題文の設問については，日米の専門家が4技能試験や英検の設問を徹底的に研究し，設問文や選択肢の平均語数も割り出したうえで，緻密に制作しました。大学入試や4技能試験，英検など，あらゆる試験に通用する，「最も汎用性が高い」と考えられる形式の設問にしているため，単に表面的な内容や語彙の知識だけを問うものではなく，4技能試験と同様に，日本語を介さず，英文の論理や大局的な意味をつかむことを重視した設問が多くなっています。

　そのほか，「音」を使った学習ができるように，すべての英文に米国人ナレーターによるリスニング音声を施してあります。学んだ英文素材を耳で確認し，音読し，定着させることで，「リーディング」だけでなく，「リスニング」の力も同時に鍛えることが可能となります。

　さらに，「語句リスト」の充実も本書が力を入れている点です。リーディングにおいては，文章を理解するための「語彙力」も極めて重要になってきます。当然，知らなかった重要単語は新たに覚えなければなりませんが，リーディングの学習中に，いちいち知らない単語を1つ1つ辞書で調べるというのは，効率的であるとはいえません。本書では，長文を読むために必要な語彙のレベルはかなり高くなってはいますが，一方で「語句リスト」を通常の長文問題集よりも充実させていますので，辞書を逐一調べる手間を省略すると同時に，「高度な語彙力」を短時間で身につけられるようになっています。

　このように，本書は，現在の入試にも未来の入試にも，そしてみなさんが将来世界で活躍するときにも役に立つ，「本物」の英語学習ができるような工夫が詰め込まれた問題集です。本書を活用したみなさんが，大学受験においても将来の英語学習においても，大きな成功を収めることを心より願い，応援しています。

安河内 哲也

本書の特長
GOOD POINTS OF THIS BOOK

1 大学入試＋4技能試験に対応

問題集のアイテム（問題文）の選択においては，「**TLU**(Target Language Use)：目標使用言語領域」の設定が非常に重要です。例えば，海外の高校・大学で講義を理解する力を試す TOEFL などの4技能試験では，TLU は **Academic**，つまり「学校で使われる英語」です。学校の教科書や講義で使われる可能性が高い英語ということになります。また，TOEIC であれば，TLU は **Business**，つまり「ビジネスパーソンが職場や生活で使用する英語」です。英検の TLU は **General**，つまり「一般的な日常生活で使用する英語」となります。Academic や Business は一般的な日常英語も含むため，General と一部重なる部分もあります。

大事なのは，**TLU が異なれば，必要となる知識や語彙も異なる**ということです。ゆえに，高校生のための問題集を開発する際にも，この TLU の設定は極めて重要

になってくるのです。

TOEFL や TEAP のような4技能試験では，TLU が **Academic** な英文が出題されます。一方，大学入試の問題文は，TLU は Academic から General にまたがっており，またその内容も形式も大学ごとに様々です。さらに，ある分野に関する特定の知識を要するものや，ある一定の年齢以上の人しか知らないような情報を前提としているケースも多々あります。よって，これらの大学入試問題をランダムに収録するだけでは，レベルも内容も設問もバラバラな，試験対策としては極めて非効率な問題集になってしまいます。

そのため，本書では，単に出題校や英文の難易度でアイテムを選ぶのではなく，「**TLU が Academic 領域であること**」「**各種4技能試験にも対応した内容であること**」「**一般的な高校生の予備知識があれば読める内容であること**」という確固とした基準を設けて，厳選を徹底しました。

また，設問*についても，日米の専門家が4技能試験や英検の設問を徹底的に研究し，あらゆる試験に通用するものを制作しました。本書を学習することで，大学入試の英文読解力が高まると「同時」に，TOEFL・英検・TEAP といった「4技能試験」の「リーディング」の力も高められるようになっています。

2 「上位版」レベル別問題集

この『英語長文 PREMIUM 問題集』シリーズは，**スタンダード**(Standard)，**アドバンスト**(Advanced)，**トップ**(Top)という3つのレベルに分かれています。これらは，日本の大学入試のレベルだけ

▲各試験のTLU（イメージ）

*設問…問題文（英語長文）のあとに設けられた質問文。（1）…（2）…や，問1…問2…などの小問のこと。

3

ではなく，**CEFR**(セファール)*という世界中の国々で英語力の指標として使われているレベルも考慮して設定されました。

下表のとおり，CEFRのレベルは下から「A1 → A2 → B1 → B2 → C1 → C2」の6つに分かれています。この各レベルにおける語句の難易度や構文の複雑さ，内容の抽象度などを考慮し，本書では厳選した60の問題文を3つのレベルに分け，おおよその目安として，Standard = B1 ～ B2, Advanced = B2, Top = B2 ～ C1（一部）となるように設定しました。これは，ベストセラー『英語長文レベル別問題集』のレベル④～⑥とほぼ同じ難度

であり，主に**B2**レベルの文章を手厚く演習できる本シリーズでリーディングのトレーニングを重ねれば，大学受験なら有名私大～難関大，英検なら準1級，TOEFL iBTなら72点以上，TEAPなら334点以上という**高度な領域**に対する効果的な演習となり，あらゆるリーディングテストに十分対応できる強靭な読解力が身につくでしょう。

また，このCEFRを基準とすることで，本書と各種4技能試験のレベル対応も目安として概ねわかります。対照表を参考にしながら，段階的に英語の学習を進めていきましょう。

CEFRと各種検定試験の対照表

難度	CEFRレベル	Can-do※	英検	TOEFL iBT	IELTS	TEAP	GTEC CBT	TOEIC (L&R)	本書の英文レベル（目安）
難 ↑	C2	抽象的で極めて複雑な文章も含め，あらゆる英文を容易に読むことができる。			9.0 | 8.5				
	C1	長く複雑な文章や，自分の専門外の文章でも理解することができる。	1級	120 | 95	8.0 | 7.0	400	1400	990 | 945	
	B2	一般的な文章や自分の専門分野の文章を，辞書を使わずに読むことができる。	準1級	94 | 72	6.5 | 5.5	399 | 334	1399 | 1250	940 | 785	Standard / Advanced / Top
	B1	新聞・雑誌の要点や，平易な英文物語の筋を理解することができる。	2級	71 | 42	5.0 | 4.0	333 | 226	1249 | 1000	780 | 550	
	A2	簡単な英語で書かれた説明文・物語文などを理解することができる。	準2級		3.0	225 | 186	999 | 700	545 | 225	
↓ 易	A1	日常生活で使われる非常に短い文章等を理解することができる。	3級 4級 5級		2.0		699	220 | 120	

※ Can-do…実際の言語を使う場面で何がどの程度できるかを段階別に記述したもの。上表は「読むこと」の一例（一部略）。

* CEFR…Common European Framework of Reference for Languages（ヨーロッパ言語共通参照枠）の略。Council of Europeが提唱した言語共通の到達度指標で，総合的な言語能力の指標として，ヨーロッパだけでなく世界中で活用され始めている。

3 「リスニング」も同時強化

　本書のCDに収録された英文音声は，多くの4技能試験で使用されるリスニング音声の速度（大学の教授が講義する速度）と同様の速度で録音してあります。これによって，リーディングの力はもちろん，アカデミックな4技能試験に対応する「リスニング」の力も同時に高めることができます。解き終わった問題文は，その後何度も音声を聞いてください。リーディングとリスニングを融合して学習することによって，リスニングはリーディングの確認・定着に，リーディングはリスニングの基礎固めになるという，2技能の学習が相乗効果を生む，加速度的且つ効率的な技能の習得が可能になるでしょう。

4 2冊分の問題を1冊に収録

　本書の本文用紙には裏写りが少ない高級用紙を使い，最高に開きの良い（机の上に広げて置くことができる）特殊製本を採用。20題もの問題を1冊に収めました。通常の長文問題集は10題程度なので，本書は，高級な用紙・製本を採用した「プレミアム」な1冊で「2冊分」のトレーニングができるという問題集になっています。

志望校レベルと本書の英文レベル対照表

難易度	志望校レベル（目安）※		本書の英文レベル（目安）	英語長文レベル別問題集（参考）※
	国公立大	私立大		
難 ↑	東京大，京都大，北海道大，東北大，名古屋大，大阪大，九州大，東京外国語大，東京工業大，一橋大，神戸大　など	早稲田大，慶應義塾大，上智大，国際基督教大	Top	レベル⑥【難関編】
	国際教養大，筑波大，千葉大，お茶の水女子，首都大学東京，東京学芸大，横浜国立大，新潟大，金沢大，広島大，熊本大，国公立大医学部　など	東京理科大，中央大（法），関西学院大，同志社大，私大医学部　など	Advanced	レベル⑤【上級編】
	岩手大，埼玉大，富山大，信州大，静岡大，岐阜大，三重大，滋賀大，大阪府立大，和歌山大，島根大，岡山大，香川大　など	明治大，青山学院大，立教大，法政大，中央大，立命館大，関西大，学習院大，津田塾大，獨協大，南山大，私大歯・薬学部　など	Standard	レベル④【中級編】
	共通テスト，その他国公立大	日本大，東洋大，駒澤大，専修大，京都産業大，近畿大，甲南大，龍谷大，成蹊大，成城大，明治学院大，國學院大，名古屋外国語大　など		レベル③【標準編】
↓ 易		大東文化大，東海大，亜細亜大，帝京大，国士舘大，創価大，拓殖大，関東学院大，桃山学院大，神戸学院大，福岡大		（レベル①・②は省略）
		共立女子短大，大妻女子短大部，日大短大部，関西外国語短大部　など		

※大学入試で出題される英文は，CEFRレベルでは概ね「B1～B2」前後の範囲になります。

＊本書のレベルや内容構成は，『英語長文レベル別問題集』（東進ブックス）のレベル④～⑥とほぼ同等です。問題文は異なるので，同レベルにおけるリーディングのトレーニングを重ねたい人は，両方学習することをおすすめします。

本書のレベル
THE LEVEL OF THIS BOOK

こんな人に最適！
- ☑ リーディングの力は標準レベルで，そこから上位を目指したい人
- ☑ 共通テストレベルの英文を「速く」「正確」に読めるようになりたい人
- ☑ 有名私大レベルの長文をきちんと読解できるようになりたい人
- ☑ 英検2級合格，TEAP225点突破を目指す人

Standardレベルの位置付け

　本書は，有名私大から早慶上智，および難関国公立大レベルを第一志望とする「中上位生」のために作られた長文問題集です。共通テストや中堅私大レベルと同等またはそれよりも少し難易度の高い有名私大などで主に出題される，国際基準で「標準的」なレベルの英文を扱うのが，このStandardレベルです。CEFRレベルでいうと概ねB1からB2にまたがる範囲なので，英検でいえば2級から準1級程度の英文難易度になります。ただ，学習の効果・効率を考慮して，問題文の語数はあえて400〜500語程度に絞ってあり，設問においても不要な「難問・奇問」が一切存在しないため，解答にあたっての難度はそこまで高くはなく，高度な英文を効率的に読解するトレーニングが何度もできるようになっています。

　なお，英検・TEAP・TOEFLといった4技能試験のリーディングパート対策としても十分機能するよう，設問は内容一致問題と空所補充問題を主としています。ただ単に表面の意味を追うのではなく，前後の文脈や筋道，パラグラフ全体の論旨にも注意しながら読み進めるようにしましょう。

「標準以上」の実力を養成

　このレベルの英文がすらすら読めるようになると，共通テストや中堅私大においてはほとんどの英文を容易に読み解くことができるようになり，かなりの高得点を狙うことができます。また，有名私大や国公立二次試験の英文についても十分に読み進めることができるレベルとなります。本書をすべて終えたら，さらに上のAdvancedレベルへと進み，高度な英文でも読み解くことができる読解力を磨いていきましょう。

※本書のレベルは，「問題文（英文）」の語彙・構造・内容などの難易度でレベル分けされており，出題大学のレベル等は一切関係ありません。

最高品質のプレミアム問題集

　本書が「PREMIUM」と名づけられた所以は，中身の品質だけではありません。表紙には持ちやすく耐久性にも優れた高級厚紙を使用。本文用紙には表面に微量の塗工を施した裏写りが少ない高級紙を用い，20題もの問題を1冊に収束させました。通常の薄めの長文問題集は10題程度なので，本書は通常の「2冊分」が収録されていることになります。

　さらに，製本方法に関しては，本のノドの奥までよく開く製本を採用し，机上における学習のしやすさを高めました。

　このように，「中」だけでなく「外」についても最高品質を追求した「PREMIUM」問題集で，みなさんの英語力も最高級なものに磨き上げていきましょう。

本書の使い方
HOW TO USE THIS BOOK

　本書には，大学入試に出題された英語長文問題が全20題（Lesson 01〜20）収録されています。各Lessonは，❶問題文→❷設問→❸解答・解説→❹構造分析／和訳（＋語句リスト）という極めてシンプルな見開き構成で進んでいきます。

　1日1題，1週間に5題（残り2日は復習）というペースで学習すれば，1ヵ月で1冊完了する分量なので，Standard → Advanced → Top へと，ハイレベルな世界でも着実にレベルアップしていきましょう。

本書で使用する記号

S＝主語　　　V＝動詞（原形）
O＝目的語　　C＝補語
※従属節の場合は S′ V′ O′ C′ を使用。
※従属節の中の従属節は SVOC を省略。

SV＝文・節（主語＋動詞）
Vp＝過去形
Vpp＝過去分詞
Ving＝現在分詞 or 動名詞
to V＝不定詞

〜＝名詞
…＝形容詞 or 副詞
……＝その他の要素（文や節など）

[ ]＝言い換え可能　　※英文中の[ ]の場合
( )＝省略可能　　　　※英文中の( )の場合
A／B＝対になる要素（品詞は関係なし）
①②③ など ＝同じ要素の並列
O(A) O(B)＝第4文型（S V O(A) O(B)）の目的語

[ ]＝名詞（のカタマリ）
▢＝修飾される名詞（のカタマリ）
< >＝形容詞（のカタマリ）・同格
( )＝副詞（のカタマリ）

❶ ▶東進が誇る多数の実力講師陣が協議を重ね，高校生の英語力を本当に伸ばす長文問題を厳選。

❷ ▶大学受験はもちろん，英検・TEAPなどの資格試験対策にもなる次世代型の設問のみを収録。

❸ ▶徹底的に無駄を排除した，シンプルで合理的な解説文。正解の根拠・理由を明示。

❹ ▶一目でわかる英文構造と，意味対応の比較に最適な直訳的和訳。豊富な語句リストも便利。

復習して次の問題へ

構造分析の記号
STRUCTURAL ANALYSIS SIGN

[名詞]の働きをするもの

▶名詞の働きをする部分は [　] で囲む。

1 動名詞

[Eating too much] is bad for your health.
[食べ過ぎること] は健康に悪い。

My sister is very good at [singing *karaoke*].
私の姉は [カラオケを歌うこと] がとても上手だ。

2 不定詞の名詞的用法

Her dream was [to become a novelist].
彼女の夢は [小説家になること] だった。

It is difficult [to understand this theory].
[この理論を理解すること] は難しい。

3 疑問詞＋不定詞

Would you tell me [how to get to the stadium]?
[どのようにして競技場へ行けばよいか] を教えていただけますか。

I didn't know [what to say].
私は [何と言ってよいのか] わからなかった。

4 that節「SがVするということ」

I think [that he will pass the test].
私は [彼がテストに合格するだろう] と思う。

It is strange [that she hasn't arrived yet].
[彼女がまだ到着していないというの] は奇妙だ。

5 if節「SがVするかどうか」

I asked her [if she would attend the party].
私は彼女に [パーティーに出席するかどうか] を尋ねた。

It is doubtful [if they will accept our offer].
[彼らが私たちの申し出を受け入れるかどうか] は疑わしい。

6 疑問詞節

Do you know [where he comes from]?
あなたは [彼がどこの出身であるか] 知っていますか。

I don't remember [what time I left home].
私は [何時に家を出たか] 覚えていません。

7 関係代名詞のwhat節

I didn't understand [what he said].
私は [彼が言うこと] を理解できなかった。

[What you need most] is a good rest.
[君に最も必要なもの] は十分な休息だ。

＜形容詞＞の働きをするもの

▶形容詞の働きをする部分を＜　＞で囲み、修飾される名詞を☐で囲む。

1 前置詞＋名詞

What is the population ＜of this city＞?
＜この市の＞ 人口 はどのくらいですか。

Look at the picture ＜on the wall＞.
＜壁に掛かっている＞ 絵 を見なさい。

2 不定詞の形容詞的用法

Today I have a lot of work ＜to do＞.
今日私は＜するべき＞ たくさんの仕事 がある。

Some people have no house ＜to live in＞.
＜住むための＞ 家 を持たない人々もいる。

3 現在分詞

The building ＜standing over there＞ is a church.
＜向こうに建っている＞ 建物 は教会です。

A woman ＜carrying a large parcel＞ got out of the bus.
＜大きな包みを抱えた＞ 女性 がバスから降りてきた。

4 過去分詞

This is a shirt ＜made in China＞.
これは＜中国で作られた＞ シャツ です。

Cars ＜parked here＞ will be removed.
＜ここに駐車された＞ 車 は撤去されます。

5 関係代名詞節

Do you know the man ＜who is standing by the gate＞?
あなたは＜門のそばに立っている＞ 男性 を知っていますか。

Is this the key ＜which you were looking for＞?
これが＜あなたが探していた＞ 鍵 ですか。

A woman ＜whose husband is dead＞ is called a widow.
＜夫が亡くなっている＞ 女性 は未亡人と呼ばれる。

6 関係副詞節

Do you remember the day ＜when we met for the first time＞?
＜私たちが初めて出会った＞ 日 をあなたは覚えていますか。

Kyoto is the city ＜where I was born＞.
京都は＜私が生まれた＞ 都市 です。

＜同格＞の働きをするもの

▶同格説明の部分を＜ ＞で囲み，説明される名詞を ▭ で囲む。

1 同格のthat節

We were surprised at |the news| ＜that he entered the hospital＞.
＜彼が入院したという＞ |知らせ| に私たちは驚いた。

There is |little chance| ＜that he will win＞.
＜彼が勝つという＞ |見込み| はほとんどない。

2 カンマによる同格補足

|Masao| , ＜my eldest son＞, is finishing high school this year.
＜私の長男である＞ |マサオ| は，今年高校を卒業する予定です。

I lived in |Louisville| , ＜the largest city in Kentucky＞.
私は＜ケンタッキー州最大の都市である＞ |ルイビル| に住んでいた。

（副詞）の働きをするもの

▶副詞の働きをする部分を（ ）で囲む。

1 前置詞＋名詞

I met my teacher (at the bookstore).
私は（本屋で）先生に会った。

I listened to music (over the radio).
私は（ラジオで）音楽を聞いた。

2 分詞構文（Ving）

(Preparing for supper), she cut her finger.
（夕食の準備をしていて）彼女は指を切った。

(Having read the newspaper), I know about the accident.
（新聞を読んだので）その事故については知っている。

3 受動分詞構文（Vpp）

(Seen from a distance), the rock looks like a human face.
（遠くから見られたとき）その岩は人間の顔のように見える。

(Shocked at the news), she fainted.
（その知らせを聞いてショックを受けたので）彼女は卒倒した。

4 従属接続詞＋ＳＶ

(When I was a child), I went to Hawaii.
（子供の頃に）私はハワイへ行った。

I didn't go to the party (because I had a cold).
（かぜをひいていたので）私はパーティーに行かなかった。

5 不定詞の副詞的用法

I was very surprised (to hear the news).
私は（その知らせを聞いて）とても驚いた。

(To drive a car), you have to get a driver's license.
（車を運転するためには）君は運転免許を取らねばならない。

特殊な記号

1 主節の挿入｛ ｝

Mr. Tanaka, {I think}, is a good teacher.
田中先生は良い教師だと｛私は思う｝。

His explanation, {it seems}, doesn't make sense.
彼の説明は意味をなさない｛ように思える｝。

2 関係代名詞主格の直後の挿入

He has a son who {people say} is a genius.
彼は天才だと｛人々が言う｝息子を持っている。

Do what {you think} is right.
正しいと｛あなたが思う｝ことをしなさい。

3 関係代名詞のas節

＊これは副詞的感覚で使用されるため，本書ではあえて（ ）の記号を使用しています。

(As is usual with him), Mike played sick.
（彼には普通のことだが）マイクは仮病を使った。

He is from Kyushu, (as you know from his accent).
（あなたが彼のなまりからわかるとおり），彼は九州出身です。

もくじ ⊕学習記録
CONTENTS

	Lesson No.	ページ	語数	制限時間	目標得点	得点	日付
STAGE-1	Lesson 01	12	438	20分	40/50点	点	月 日
	Lesson 02	22	450	20分	40/50点	点	月 日
	Lesson 03	32	355	20分	40/50点	点	月 日
	Lesson 04	42	536	20分	40/50点	点	月 日
	Lesson 05	52	478	20分	40/50点	点	月 日
STAGE-2	Lesson 06	64	443	20分	40/50点	点	月 日
	Lesson 07	74	489	20分	40/50点	点	月 日
	Lesson 08	84	498	20分	40/50点	点	月 日
	Lesson 09	94	518	20分	40/50点	点	月 日
	Lesson 10	104	442	20分	40/50点	点	月 日
STAGE-3	Lesson 11	116	403	20分	40/50点	点	月 日
	Lesson 12	126	392	20分	40/50点	点	月 日
	Lesson 13	136	309	20分	40/50点	点	月 日
	Lesson 14	146	358	20分	40/50点	点	月 日
	Lesson 15	156	470	20分	40/50点	点	月 日
STAGE-4	Lesson 16	168	323	20分	40/50点	点	月 日
	Lesson 17	178	419	20分	40/50点	点	月 日
	Lesson 18	188	363	20分	40/50点	点	月 日
	Lesson 19	198	406	20分	40/50点	点	月 日
	Lesson 20	208	335	20分	40/50点	点	月 日

＊問題を解いたあとは得点と日付を記入し，CD音声を何度も聴きましょう。1日1題，1週間に5題（残り2日は復習などにあてる）というペースで学習すれば，1ヵ月で1冊が完了します。

Premium Reading Workbook

Standard
STAGE-1

Lesson 01–05

Johns Hopkins is America's first research university, founded on the belief that teaching and research are interdependent, and that a modern university must do both well. Today, we remain a world leader in both teaching and research, with more than 21,000 undergraduate and graduate students studying with esteemed faculty members across nine world-class academic divisions.

Johns Hopkins University

Lesson 01
問題文

単語数 ▶ 438 words
制限時間 ▶ 20 分
目標得点 ▶ 40 / 50点

■ Read the passage and answer the following questions.

　For centuries, Native Americans living in what is now the United States and Canada lived close to nature, using only what they needed from the natural environment in order to survive. But when Europeans arrived on the continent, they saw an abundance of materials that they could use and sell. They cut down the forests, killed animals for sport, and used farming methods that allowed the wind and rain to erode the soil. To many of the new settlers, it must have seemed that there was an endless supply of forests, animals, and land.

　By the 1870s, settlers were moving west in astonishing numbers. It was at this time that a small group of people became concerned about protecting the magnificent scenery and abundant wildlife in an area that is now part of the states of Wyoming, Montana, and Idaho. This part of the country had geysers*, hot springs, and waterfalls; there were also snow-covered mountains, clear lakes, and huge trees. The group of concerned citizens worried that unless these (x)natural wonders were protected by the government, their descendants would never have a chance to see them. In 1872, they convinced the U.S. government to make the area into a national park. Called Yellowstone National Park, it was the country's first national park.

　When Yellowstone National Park was created, no one gave much thought to how the park would be managed, who would actually protect it, and where the money to take care of it would come from. In fact, during the park's first few years, no money at all was provided to take care of it. And with no one assigned to protect the area, vandalism* by curious visitors and the killing of wildlife within the park's boundary became serious problems. Finally, in 1883, the government asked the U.S. Army to protect the park, and for the next 30 years, it remained under the army's control. In the final years of the 19th century, more national parks were established, hunting was banned in the parks, and a few roads were built through the parks.

Realizing that the national parks needed to be managed and protected, the U.S. government created the National Park System in 1912. The goal of the park system was to create and manage parks that would preserve and protect unique natural landscapes, wildlife habitats, and sites of historic or cultural significance.

Today, the U.S. National Park System is made up of 375 parks, covering more than 300,000 square kilometers of land. The parks can be used for camping, hiking, fishing and boating. Scientists, naturalists, and historians provide information, give talks, and lead guided walks.

(Patricia Ackert / Linda Lee 著 *Concepts & Comments*, Third Edition, Thomson & Heinle)

* geyser（間欠泉）　vandalism（破壊行為）

Lesson 01
設問

(1) What is mainly being discussed?

　1 The colonization of the American West

　2 The management of natural ecosystems

　3 The training of government officials

　4 The animals living in captivity

(2) According to paragraph 2, what was a group of 1870s citizens concerned about?

　1 States were over-competing for resources.

　2 Wildlife were escaping from parks.

　3 Some land features might disappear.

　4 Scenery was becoming more unattractive.

(3) The phrase "natural wonders" in line (X) is closest in meaning to

　1 amazing people.

　2 unique locations.

　3 remote environments.

　4 special opportunities.

(4) What is NOT a problem mentioned in paragraph 3?

　1　Lack of funds

　2　Incidents of vandalism

　3　Killings of animals

　4　Development of homes

(5) According to paragraph 3, what assignment was the U.S. Army given in 1883?

　1　Securing a region

　2　Building roads

　3　Finding more parks

　4　Protecting governors

No.	(1)	(2)	(3)	(4)	(5)
配点	10点	10点	10点	10点	10点
解答欄					

解 答 用 紙

Lesson 01
解答・解説

（1） 主に議論されていることは何か。
1 アメリカ西部の植民地化
② 自然生態系の管理
3 政府関係者の訓練
4 捕らえられて生活している動物

解説▶本文は「何世紀にもわたり……生き残るために必要とするものだけを自然環境の中から用いてきた」という導入で始まり，続く段落以降では，**国立公園を創設し，管理することで自然環境を守ろうとする活動**について述べられている。よって，**2** が正解とわかる。

（2） 第2段落によると，1870年代の市民のある団体が懸念していたことは何か。
1 州は資源を求めて過剰な競争をしていた。
2 野生動物は公園から逃げていた。
③ いくつかの地形は消滅するかもしれなかった。
4 景色がより魅力のないものになりつつあった。

解説▶第2段落第4文「憂慮する市民の団体はこのような自然の驚異は政府により守られない限り，彼らの子孫たちはそれらを見る機会がなくなってしまうだろうと心配した」より，彼らは**自然が失われてしまうことを懸念していた**ことがわかる。よって，**3** が正解となる。

（3） 下線部(X)の「natural wonders」という表現は，……に最も意味が近い。
1 すばらしい人々
② 特有の場所
3 人里離れた環境
4 特別な機会

解説▶「憂慮する市民の団体はこのような natural wonders は政府により守られない限り，彼らの子孫たちはそれらを見る機会がなくなってしまうだろうと心配した」が文意。そこで，下線部直前の these に注目したい。these は前文で述べられた**政府によって守られるべきもの**，つまり**間欠泉，温泉，滝，雪に覆われた山々，澄んだ湖，巨大な木々**などを指していることがわかる。よって，**2** が正解とわかる。

(4) 第3段落で述べられていない問題点は何か。
1 資金不足
2 破壊行為事件
3 動物の殺害
④ 生息地の開拓

解説 ▶ **1** は第3段落第1文後半「どこからそれ（公園）を管理するための資金を得るのか」，**2** は第3文前半「訪問者による破壊行為」，**3** は第3文後半「野生生物の殺害」でそれぞれ述べられている。よって，**4** が正解となる。

(5) 第3段落によると，1883年にアメリカ軍に与えられた任務は何だったか。
① 地域を守ること
2 道路を建設すること
3 もっと公園を見つけること
4 知事を守ること

解説 ▶ 第3段落第4文前半「1883年に政府はアメリカ軍にその公園を保護するように求め」から，**1** が正解とわかる。

No.	(1)	(2)	(3)	(4)	(5)
配点	10点	10点	10点	10点	10点
解答欄	2	3	2	4	1

正解

| 得点 | （1回目） /50点 | （2回目） | （3回目） | CHECK YOUR LEVEL | 0〜30点 ➡ Work harder!
31〜40点 ➡ OK!
41〜50点 ➡ Way to go! |

Lesson 01
構造分析

[　] = 名詞　　□ = 修飾される名詞　　< > = 形容詞・同格　　(　) = 副詞
S = 主語　V = 動詞　O = 目的語　C = 補語　′ = 従節

❶ (For centuries), [Native Americans <living (in [what is (now) the United States and Canada])> lived (close to nature), (using (only) [what they needed] (from the natural environment) (in order to survive)). But (when Europeans arrived (on the continent)), they saw [an abundance of materials] <that they could use and sell>. They cut (down) the forests, killed animals (for sport), and used [farming methods] <that allowed the wind and rain (to erode the soil)>. (To many of the new settlers), it must have seemed [that there was [an endless supply] <of forests, animals, and land>].

❷ (By the 1870s), settlers were moving (west) (in astonishing numbers). It was (at this time) that a small group of people became concerned (about protecting the magnificent scenery and abundant wildlife (in [an area] <that is now [part] <of the states of Wyoming, Montana, and Idaho>>)). [This part] <of the country> had geysers, hot springs, and waterfalls; there were (also) snow-covered mountains, clear lakes, and huge trees. [The group] <of concerned citizens> worried [that (unless these natural wonders were protected (by the government)), their descendants would (never) have [a chance] <to see them>]. (In 1872), they convinced the U.S. government (to make the area (into a national park)). (Called Yellowstone National Park), it was the country's first national park.

【和訳】

❶ 何世紀にもわたり，現在のアメリカとカナダに住んでいたアメリカ先住民は自然と密接に関わって生活し，生き残るために必要とするものだけを自然環境の中から用いてきた。しかし，ヨーロッパ人がその大陸に到着したとき，彼らは自分たちが使用でき，売れるものが豊富にあるとわかった。彼らは森を切り倒し，ふざけて動物を殺し，風雨が土壌を浸食するのを可能にするような農業の方法を用いた。新しく移住した多くの者にとって，森林や動物や土地は無限に供給されるように思えたにちがいない。

❷ 1870年代までに，開拓移民たちは驚くべき人数で西へと移動していった。わずかな集団が，現在のワイオミング州，モンタナ州そしてアイダホ州の一部の地域におけるその荘厳な景色と豊富な野生生物の保護について気にかけるようになったのはこのときであった。国のこの地域には，間欠泉，温泉，滝があり，また雪に覆われた山々や，澄んだ湖，そして巨大な木々があった。憂慮する市民の団体はこのような自然の驚異は政府により守られない限り，彼らの子孫たちはそれらを見る機会がなくなってしまうだろうと心配した。1872年に，彼らはアメリカ政府にその地域を国立公園とするよう説得した。（その地域は）イエローストーン国立公園と呼ばれ，その国の最初の国立公園となった。

重要語句リスト

語句	品詞	意味
in order to V	熟	Vするために
survive	動	生き残る，切り抜ける
continent	名	大陸
an abundance of ~	熟	豊富な，大量の~
cut down ~	熟	~を切り倒す
forest	名	森
for sport	熟	ふざけて，冗談に
farming	名	農業
method	名	方法
allow ~ to V	熟	~がVするのを可能にする
erode	動	浸食する
soil	名	土壌，土地
many of ~	熟	多くの~
settler	名	開拓移民
it must have Vpp that ⋯⋯		⋯⋯はVだったに違いない
endless	形	無限の，終わりのない
supply	名	供給
land	名	土地，大陸
astonishing	形	驚くべき
it is ~ that S V	熟	SがVするのは~である
at this time	熟	このとき，現時点では
a group of ~	熟	~の集団
become concerned about ~		~を気にかける，~を心配する
magnificent	形	荘厳な，素晴らしい
scenery	名	景色，風景
abundant	形	豊富な，大量の
wildlife	名	野生生物
area	名	地域
part of ~	熟	~の一部
state	名	州，国家，状態
hot spring	名	温泉
waterfall	名	滝
snow-covered	形	雪に覆われた
huge	形	巨大な，大量の
concerned	形	憂慮する
citizen	名	市民
unless ⋯⋯	接	⋯⋯しない限り
wonder	名	驚異，驚き
government	名	政府
descendant	名	子孫
have a chance	熟	機会がある
convince ~ to V	熟	~をVするように説得する

❸ (When Yellowstone National Park was created), no one gave much thought (to [how the park would be managed], [who would (actually) protect it], and [where the money <to take care of it> would come from]). (In fact), (during the park's first few years), no money (at all) was provided (to take care of it). And (with no one assigned (to protect the area)), vandalism <by curious visitors> and the killing <of wildlife> <within the park's boundary> became serious problems. (Finally), (in 1883), the government asked the U.S. Army (to protect the park), and (for the next 30 years), it remained (under the army's control). (In the final years <of the 19th century>), more national parks were established, hunting was banned (in the parks), and a few roads were built (through the parks).

❹ (Realizing [that the national parks needed to be managed and protected]), the U.S. government created the National Park System (in 1912). The goal <of the park system> was [to create and manage parks <that would preserve and protect unique natural landscapes, wildlife habitats, and sites <of historic or cultural significance>>].

❺ (Today), the U.S. National Park System is made (up) (of 375 parks), (covering more than 300,000 square kilometers of land). The parks can be used (for camping, hiking, fishing and boating). Scientists, naturalists, and historians provide information, give talks, and lead guided walks.

❸ イエローストーン国立公園が創設されたとき，どのようにその公園が管理されるのか，実際，誰がそれを保護するのか，そしてどこからそれ（公園）を管理するための資金を得るのかについて，誰もあまり考えていなかった。実際，その公園が創設された最初の数年間，その公園を管理するために，一切の資金も提供されなかった。そして，誰もその地域を保護するよう任命されなかったので，好奇心の強い訪問者による破壊行為やその公園の境界内での野生生物の殺害が，深刻な問題になった。とうとう，1883年に政府はアメリカ軍にその公園を保護するように求め，そこから30年間その公園は軍の管理下に置かれたままであった。19世紀の終わりの数年で，より多くの国立公園が設立され，その公園内では狩りが禁止され，公園内を通り抜けるいくつかの道が作られた。

❹ 国立公園は管理され，保護されなければならないとわかり，アメリカ政府は1912年に国立公園システムを作った。そのシステムの目的は独特な自然の景観，野生動物の生息地，そして歴史的，文化的に重要な場所を保存し保護する公園の創設と管理であった。

❺ 今日，国立公園システムは375の公園で成り立っており，300,000平方キロメートル以上を占めている。その公園はキャンプ，ハイキング，魚釣りや，ボート遊びに使われる。科学者，動植物研究家，歴史家が情報を提供し，話をし，ガイドツアーを行っている。

☐ make A into B	熟	A を B にする
☐ national park	名	国立公園
☐ create	動	創設する
☐ manage	動	管理する，運営する
☐ actually	副	実際，実は
☐ take care of ~	熟	~を管理する，~の世話をする
☐ in fact	熟	実際
☐ during	前	~の間に
☐ first few years	熟	最初の数年
☐ no ~ at all	熟	少しの~もない，全く~がない
☐ provide	動	提供する，供給する
☐ assign	動	任命する
☐ curious	形	好奇心の強い
☐ killing	名	殺すこと
☐ within	前	~内で
☐ boundary	名	境界（線）
☐ serious	形	深刻な，重大な
☐ finally	副	とうとう，ついに
☐ ask ~ to V	熟	~に V するよう求める
☐ remain C	動	C のままでいる，残る
☐ under one's control	熟	（人の）管理下に置かれて，統制されて
☐ army	名	軍
☐ establish	動	設立する，築き上げる
☐ hunting	名	狩猟
☐ ban	動	禁止する
☐ build	動	作る，建てる
☐ through	前	~を通り抜けて，~を通して
☐ realize	動	わかる
☐ need to V	熟	V しなければならない，V する必要がある
☐ preserve	動	保存する，保護する
☐ unique	形	独特な
☐ landscape	名	景観，風景
☐ habitat	名	生息地
☐ significance	名	重要性
☐ be made up of ~	熟	~で成り立っている
☐ square	名	平方
☐ boating	名	ボート遊び
☐ give talk	熟	話をする
☐ guided walk	熟	ガイドツアー

Lesson 02
問題文

■ Read the passage and answer the following questions.

　The societies of Japan and the United States are quite different and because of these differences, Japanese and American people often have a difficult time communicating. This difficulty is not only based on the mastery of the other's language. It is based on different sets of social conventions* and the underlying stories for these conventions. By underlying stories, I mean our cultures' unspoken assumptions.

　One example of social convention can be seen when visiting an acquaintance's* house. In the United States, it is not unusual for friends, or even co-workers, to drop by your house. While certainly we have formal dinners or visits as well, I'm (1) the custom of stopping by more casually (although it is generally considered rude to arrive unannounced). In Japan, it is (2) to visit a friend's house this casually, and extremely rare for a co-worker to do so.

　We could say that once you get to the friend's/co-worker's house how you might expect to be treated would be different. In Japan, you would probably be shown a considerable amount of deference*, treated as an honored guest. In the United States, things would be more casual, and you might be treated almost as a family member. This leads us to underlying stories. In Japan, the underlying story in this social situation is that "the other person is to be treated as (3), and with great respect." In the United States, the story is that "we are equals, and very relaxed with each other."

If we take this (4) further, on entering a friend's house in a casual visit in the United States, the host may say something like "Grab a seat anywhere," or he/she may not even pay attention to where you sit. This continues the idea that "You are a near-family member." In Japan, the host would likely show you to a seat, since the underlying notion is "You are an honored guest."

Another example of social convention is the use of speech in the two cultures. In Japan, during a discussion it might be considered (5) to listen silently to the other's opinion, but in the United States, a person who does not contribute their opinion to a discussion might be considered boring. Generally speaking in the United States, the social convention is to offer opinions, whereas in Japan it may be to stay silent. The underlying story for the former here is "we all have valuable opinions," and in the latter "I'm respecting you by listening to your opinion."

To enhance intercultural communication it is important to understand the other's social conventions, and even more important to understand the underlying stories on which these conventions are based.

(Adapted from Shukan ST on line. July 25, 2008)

* convention (しきたり，慣習)　　acquaintance (知り合い，知人)
deference (尊敬，敬意)

Lesson 02
設問

Choose the best word or phrase from among the four choices to fill each gap.

(1) **1** referring to **2** passing up
       3 based on   **4** allowing to

(2) **1** very soon   **2** more unclear
       3 rather unusual **4** so short

(3) **1** a reaction **2** an asset
       3 a link   **4** a superior

(4) **1** success   **2** legend
       3 illustration **4** history

(5) **1** highlighted **2** flexible
       3 respectful **4** generous

Lesson 02 (2/5) 問題文→**設問**→解答・解説→構造分析

Lesson 02

解 答 用 紙					
No.	(1)	(2)	(3)	(4)	(5)
配点	10点	10点	10点	10点	10点
解答欄					

Lesson 02 解答・解説

(1) ① 言及している　　　２ 断っている
　　 ３ もとづいている　　４ 許している

　　解説▶ 第２段落は第１文より，知人の家を訪ねるときの社会的慣習の一例を述べた段落であるとわかるため，第２文より「アメリカ合衆国では，友人や同僚でさえ，家に立ち寄ることは普通である」という具体例が展開されることが予測できる。よって，「確かに，形式ばった夕食や形式ばった訪問の場合もあるだろうが，私はより何気なく立ち寄る習慣に（　１　）」は形式ばった訪問ではなく，何気ない訪問という習慣についての具体例を述べるという流れとなるのが自然なため，**1** が正解となる。

(2) 　１ すぐに　　　　　２ より曖昧な
　　 ③ いくぶん珍しい　　４ 非常に短い

　　解説▶ 第２段落では「アメリカ合衆国」と「日本」の対比関係に注目。第２文ではアメリカ合衆国では知人の家に立ち寄ることが普通であると述べられているため，**アメリカ合衆国では普通だが，日本では珍しい**という流れになることが推測できる。また，A and B は A と B に同じ意味の語句や節を並べる働きがあるため，「A：日本では，こんなにも何気なく友人の家を訪れることは（　２　）」and「B：ましてや同僚がそうすることはきわめてまれだ」の関係から（　２　）は「まれ」のイメージを含む語句，つまり正解は **3** と判断することができる。

(3) 　１ 反応　　　　　　２ 財産
　　 ３ つながり　　　　④ 優れた人

　　解説▶ 第３段落はどのようにもてなされるかに対する期待について述べられた段落である。日本での期待に注目すると，第２文より「大切なお客としてもてなされ，おそらくかなりの敬意を示されるだろう」とある。空所を含む文「相手は，かなりの尊敬をもって，（自分より）（　３　）として扱われるべきである」は，この文を言い換えた内容であるため，「**大切なお客＝プラスイメージを持つ人**」＝（　３　）となり，**4** が正解となる。

(4) 1 成功　　　　　　　　　2 伝説
　　 ③ 例　　　　　　　　　　4 歴史

解説▶空所前の this に注目。this は前で述べられた内容を指すことができる。第2～3段落は**社会的慣習の一例が述べられた段落**であるため，**3**が正解とわかる。また，第5段落「社会的慣習の別の例は」という表現からも，第2～4段落では「社会的慣習の一例」が述べられていたことがわかる。

(5) 1 目立った　　　　　　　2 融通のきく
　　 ③ 礼儀正しい　　　　　　4 気前のよい

解説▶第5段落は第1文より**日本とアメリカ合衆国における発言の仕方の社会的慣習の例について述べた段落**とわかる。ここでも日本とアメリカ合衆国の**対比関係**に注目する。「日本では，討論の間，他人の意見を静かに聞くことが（ 5 ）とされているだろう」「アメリカ合衆国では，討論で自分の意見を述べない人は，退屈だと思われるだろう」の関係から，**日本：静か＝プラスイメージ，アメリカ合衆国：静か＝マイナスイメージ**となることがわかる。よって，**3**が正解。**2**や**4**もプラスイメージを持つが，「発言の仕方」とは無関係である。

正解

No.	(1)	(2)	(3)	(4)	(5)
配点	10点	10点	10点	10点	10点
解答欄	**1**	**3**	**4**	**3**	**3**

| 得点 | （1回目） /50点 | （2回目） | （3回目） | CHECK YOUR LEVEL | 0～30点 ➡ Work harder!
31～40点 ➡ OK!
41～50点 ➡ Way to go! |

Lesson 02
構造分析

[ ]＝名詞　□＝修飾される名詞　< >＝形容詞・同格　( )＝副詞
S＝主語　V＝動詞　O＝目的語　C＝補語　'＝従節

❶ The societies <of Japan and the United States> are (quite) different and (because of these differences), Japanese and American people (often) have a difficult time <communicating>. This difficulty is (not only) based (on the mastery <of the other's language>). It is based (on different sets of social conventions and the underlying stories <for these conventions>). (By underlying stories), I mean our cultures' unspoken assumptions.

❷ One example <of social convention> can be seen (when visiting an acquaintance's house). (In the United States), it is (not) unusual (for friends, or even co-workers), [to drop by your house]. (While (certainly) we have formal dinners or visits (as well)), I'm referring (to the custom <of stopping by more casually>) (although it is generally considered rude to arrive unannounced). (In Japan), it is (rather) unusual [to visit a friend's house (this casually)], and extremely rare (for a co-worker) [to do so].

❸ We could say [that (once you get to the friend's/co-worker's house) [how you might expect to be treated] would be different]. (In Japan), you would (probably) be shown a considerable amount <of deference>, (treated (as an honored guest)). (In the United States), things would be more casual, and you might be treated (almost) (as a family member). This leads us (to underlying stories). (In Japan), the underlying story (in this social situation) is [that "the other person is to be treated (as a superior), and (with great respect)]." (In the United States), the story is [that "we are equals, and very relaxed (with each other)]."

【和訳】

❶ 日本とアメリカ合衆国の社会は非常に異なっており，こうした違いのために，日本人とアメリカ人はしばしば意思疎通するのが困難なときを過ごすものである。この困難は，相手の言語の熟達にもとづいているだけではない。それは（その困難は）一連の社会的慣習の相違とこうした慣習の裏に隠された意味にもとづいている。この裏に隠された意味によって，私は我々の文化の暗黙の前提を示したい。

❷ 社会的慣習の一例は，知人の家を訪ねるときに見られる。アメリカ合衆国では，友人や同僚でさえ，家に立ち寄ることは普通である。確かに，形式ばった夕食や形式ばった訪問の場合もあるだろうが，私はより何気なく立ち寄る習慣に言及している（突然の訪問は失礼だと一般的に考えられているが）。日本では，こんなにも何気なく友人の家を訪れることはいくぶん珍しいし，ましてや同僚がそうすることはきわめてまれである。

❸ いったん友人や同僚の家に着くと，自分がどのようにもてなされるかに対する期待は（日本とアメリカ合衆国では）異なると言えるかもしれない。日本では，大切なお客としてもてなされ，おそらくかなりの敬意を示されるだろう。アメリカ合衆国では，物事はあまり形式ばらず，（訪問した人は）家族の一員のように扱われるかもしれない。これは，私たちを裏に隠された意味へとつなげる。日本では，この社会的状況の裏に隠された意味は，「相手は，かなりの尊敬をもって，（自分より）優れた人として扱われるべきである」ということである。アメリカ合衆国では，「私たちは平等で，お互いに非常に打ち解けている」という意味になる。

重要語句リスト

difficulty	图 困難
be based on ～	熟 ～にもとづいている
mastery	图 熟達
sets of ～	熟 一連の～
underlying	形 隠された，基礎をなす
mean	動 言おうとする，意味する
unspoken	形 暗黙の
assumption	图 前提，仮定
it is … for O to V	熟 ～にとってVすることは…だ
unusual	形 普通ではない，まれな
even	副 ～でさえ
co-worker	图 同僚
drop by ～	熟 ～に立ち寄る
while S V	接 SがVだけれども
certainly	副 確かに
formal	形 形式ばった，公式の
as well	熟 その上，同様に
refer to ～	熟 ～に言及する
custom	图 習慣
stop by	熟 立ち寄る
casually	副 何気なく，気軽に
although	接 だけれども，にもかかわらず
generally	副 一般に，概して
consider	動 よく考える，熟考する
unannounced	熟 突然に，発表なしに
rather	副 いくぶん，むしろ
extremely	副 きわめて
get to ～	熟 ～に着く
how S V	熟 どのようにSがVするか
treat	動 もてなす，扱う
show	動 示す，現れる
considerable	形 かなりの
a … amount of ～	熟 …な量の～
honored	形 大切な，名誉ある
guest	图 客
lead A to B	熟 AをBへとつなげる
superior	图 優れた人
respect	图 尊敬
equal	图 対等の人
relaxed	形 打ち解けた
each other	熟 お互い

❹ If we take this illustration further, on entering a friend's house in a casual visit in the United States, the host may say something like "Grab a seat anywhere," or he/she may not (even) pay attention to where you sit. This continues the idea that "You are a near-family member." In Japan, the host would likely show you to a seat, since the underlying notion is "You are an honored guest."

❺ Another example of social convention is the use of speech in the two cultures. In Japan, during a discussion it might be considered respectful to listen silently to the other's opinion, but in the United States, a person who does not contribute their opinion to a discussion might be considered boring. Generally speaking in the United States, the social convention is to offer opinions, whereas in Japan it may be to stay silent. The underlying story for the former here is ["we all have valuable opinions,"] and in the latter ["I'm respecting you by listening to your opinion."]

❻ To enhance intercultural communication it is important to understand the other's social conventions, and even more important to understand the underlying stories on which these conventions are based.

❹ この例をさらに深めると，アメリカ合衆国では，形式ばらずに友人の家を訪れるとすぐに，その家主は「どこでも座って」というようなことを言い，訪問した人がどこに座るかに気を配りさえしないかもしれない。これは，「あなたは家族みたいな存在だ」という考えの延長にある。日本では，裏に隠された考えは「あなたは大切なお客だ」なので，家主はおそらくあなたを席へと案内するだろう。

❺ 社会的慣習の別の例は，この2つの文化における発言の仕方である。日本では，討論の間，他人の意見を静かに聞くことが礼儀正しいとされているだろうが，アメリカ合衆国では，討論で自分の意見を述べない人は，退屈だと思われるだろう。アメリカ合衆国では一般的に言って，その社会的慣習は意見を述べることであり，一方で，日本では，静かにしていることであるのかもしれない。ここでの前者（アメリカ人）の裏に隠された意味は，「我々は皆価値のある意見を持っている」であり，後者（日本人）の意味は，「あなたの意見を聞くことであなたを尊敬している」である。

❻ 異文化間のコミュニケーションをより良くするためには，相手の社会的慣習を理解することが重要であり，またこうした慣習にもとづく裏に隠された意味を理解することがさらに重要である。

□ illustration	名 例，説明
□ on Ving	熟 Vするとすぐに
□ host	名 家主
□ grab a seat	熟 席に座る
□ anywhere	副 どこでも
□ pay attention to ~	熟 ~に気を配る，~に注意を払う
□ continue	動 延長する，続く
□ likely	副 おそらく，~しそうである
□ show A to B	熟 AをBへ案内する
□ since S V	接 SがVなので
□ notion	名 考え
□ use	名 使用
□ speech	名 話し方，演説
□ during	前 ~の間に
□ discussion	名 討論
□ respectful	形 礼儀正しい
□ silently	副 静かに
□ opinion	名 意見
□ contribute	動 述べる，貢献する
□ boring	形 退屈な
□ generally speaking	熟 一般的に言って
□ offer	動 述べる，提案する
□ whereas	接 一方で，ところが
□ silent	形 静かな，無声の
□ former	名 前者
□ valuable	形 価値のある
□ latter	名 後者
□ enhance	動 より良くする，高める
□ intercultural	形 異文化間の

Lesson 03
問題文

■ Read the passage and answer the following questions.

　Have you ever had the experience of hearing a song playing in your head and you couldn't stop it?　In fact, many people have at some time in their life.　This phenomenon is known as *stuck-song syndrome, sticky music*, or more commonly, an *earworm*.　Scientists have identified a set of triggers that seem to cause tunes to pop into people's heads and stay there.　The most common trigger is when you have heard a song recently.　A song may also stick in your head if you hear it repeatedly.

　But sometimes a song will pop into your head even when you haven't heard it for a long time.　In this case, something in your current situation may trigger the memory.　One common cause of an earworm is stress.　There are many reports of people frequently hearing a song before taking important examinations or tests.　The same song might return at other times of stress.　There are various theories that may explain why this happens.　Earworms may be part of a larger phenomenon called *involuntary memory*, which includes the desire to eat a particular food after the idea has popped into your head, or suddenly thinking of a friend you've not seen for ages.

　There are a couple of reasons why this might happen with music.　One is that music is often recorded in a very personal and emotional way, and personal or emotional connections are retrieved better from memory.　Some experts suggest that music may remain in our heads because it is important for humans to remember information. Modern humans have been around for about 200,000 years, but since written language was invented only around 5,000 years ago, people memorized important information through songs. The combination of rhythm, rhyme, and melody make songs easier to recall than words alone.

So, how can we turn off earworms? Some suggest that just thinking of another song will push out the first one. Others suggest that everyday activities help, like going for a run, or doing a crossword puzzle. In fact, anything which can distract our brain from having to "listen" to the same song repeatedly may help.

Lesson 03
設問

(1) According to the author, scientists have

　　1 excluded psychological triggers as a cause of earworms.

　　2 identified music styles that most easily remain in one's head.

　　3 pinpointed factors that cause the brain to repeat a function.

　　4 established why some human memories are actually false.

(2) Which of the following is an example of involuntary memory?

　　1 Dreaming of a difficult test that one took recently

　　2 Confusing old and new information in a presentation

　　3 Recalling the wrong words to a well-known song

　　4 Wanting to contact a nearly-forgotten classmate

(3) What is true according to paragraph 3?

　　1 Some forms of music are difficult to properly record.

　　2 Emotions can block access to important thoughts.

　　3 Written language was developed before melodies.

　　4 Songs once acted as ways to pass on information.

(4) Select the TWO answer choices that are recommendations to "turn off" earworms, based on the discussion of the topic in paragraph 4. To receive credit, you must select TWO answers.

1 Listening to the same song repeatedly

2 Starting to do an exercise

3 Pushing out any distractions

4 Solving a complex task

No.	(1)	(2)	(3)	(4)
配点	10点	10点	10点	20点
解答欄				

解 答 用 紙

Lesson 03
解答・解説

(1) 筆者によると，科学者たちは
1 イヤーワームの原因として心理的誘因を除外してきた。
2 人の頭に最も容易に残る音楽様式を明らかにしてきた。
③ 脳に，ある機能を繰り返させる要因を正確に把握してきた。
4 なぜ人間の記憶の中には実際は誤っているものがあるのかを立証してきた。

解説▶ 第1段落第4文「**科学者たちは，楽曲が人々の頭の中でふと浮かび，そこにとどまることを引き起こすように思われる一連の誘因を明らかにしてきた**」から，**3** が正解とわかる。**1** は第2段落にイヤーワームの原因の1つはストレスであることが記されているため，心理的誘因を除外してはいないことがわかる。**2**・**4** については無記述。

(2) 意志によらない記憶の例は以下のどれか。
1 最近受けた難しいテストの夢を見ること
2 プレゼンテーションで旧情報と新情報を混同すること
3 よく知っている歌の間違った歌詞を思い出すこと
④ ほぼ忘れていた同級生と連絡をとりたがること

解説▶ involuntary memory（意志によらない記憶）については第2段落第7文に記されている。続く「which」以下で説明が加えられているが，その中で「**突然，長い間会っていない友人のことを考えることを含む**」とあるため，**4** が正解とわかる。

(3) 第3段落によると，どれが正しいか。
1 音楽様式の中には正確に録音するのが難しいものがある。
2 感情は重要な考えに近づく手段を妨害する可能性がある。
3 書き言葉はメロディーより前に発達した。
④ 歌はかつて，情報伝達法の役割を果たしていた。

解説▶ 第4文「現生人類は約20万年の間存在しているが，書き言葉はほんの5,000年ほど前に考案されたので，**人々は歌を通して重要な情報を記憶した**」の後半部分から，**4** が正解とわかる。**1**・**2** については無記述。**3** は第4文の後半部分から，メロディーの方が書き言葉より前に現れていることがわかる。

(4) 第4段落のトピックに関する考察にもとづき、イヤーワームを「止める」のに推奨される選択肢を2つ選べ。得点するためには2つの正解を選ばなくてはならない。
1 同じ歌を繰り返し聴くこと
② 運動を始めること
3 気をそらすものをどれでも排除すること
④ 複雑な課題を解決すること

|解説|▶第3文「また走ったり、クロスワードパズルに取り組んだりというような毎日の活動が役立つ」から、**2** や **4** のような活動が推奨されていると考えることができる。

	正 解				
No.	(1)	(2)	(3)	(4)	
配点	10点	10点	10点	20点	
解答欄	3	4	4	2	4

| 得点 | (1回目) /50点 | (2回目) | (3回目) | CHECK YOUR LEVEL | 0〜30点 ➡ *Work harder!*
31〜40点 ➡ *OK!*
41〜50点 ➡ *Way to go!* |

Lesson 03
構造分析

[　]＝名詞　　□＝修飾される名詞　　＜　＞＝形容詞・同格　　(　)＝副詞
S＝主語　V＝動詞　O＝目的語　C＝補語　'＝従節

❶ Have you (ever) had the experience <of hearing a song <playing (in your head)> and you couldn't stop it? (In fact), many people have (at some time) (in their life). This phenomenon is known (*as stuck-song syndrome, sticky music*, or (more commonly), an *earworm*). Scientists have identified a set of triggers <that seem to cause tunes (to pop (into people's heads) and stay (there))>. The most common trigger is [when you have heard a song (recently)]. A song may (also) stick (in your head) (if you hear it (repeatedly)).

❷ But (sometimes) a song will pop (into your head) (even) (when you haven't heard it (for a long time)). (In this case), something <in your current situation> may trigger the memory. One common cause <of an earworm> is stress. There are many reports <of people <(frequently) hearing a song> (before taking important examinations or tests)>. The same song might return (at other times <of stress>). There are various theories <that may explain [why this happens]>. Earworms may be part <of a larger phenomenon <called *involuntary memory*>>, (which includes the desire <to eat a particular food> (after the idea has popped (into your head)), or (suddenly) thinking (of a friend <you've not seen (for ages)>)).

【和訳】

❶ 今までに頭の中で歌が流れていて，それを止めることができないという経験をしたことがあるだろうか。実際，多くの人が人生のどこかでそうした経験があるはずだ。この現象は「曲がこびりついている症候群（stuck-song syndrome）」「こびりついた音楽（sticky music）」，もしくはより一般的に「イヤーワーム（earworm）」として知られている。科学者たちは，楽曲が人々の頭の中でふと浮かび，そこにとどまることを引き起こすように思われる一連の誘因を明らかにしてきた。最も一般的な誘因は，歌を聞いたばかりのときである。繰り返し聞けば，歌はまた頭の中に残るかもしれない。

❷ しかし，時々歌は，長い間聞いていないときでさえ，頭の中でふと浮かぶだろう。この場合，現在の状況における何かが，記憶を呼び覚ますのかもしれない。イヤーワームの一般的な原因の1つはストレスである。重要な試験やテストを受ける前に，頻繁に音楽を聞く人々に関する報告がたくさんある。同じ曲がストレスを感じた別の機会に戻ってくるのかもしれない。なぜこのようなことが起こるのかを説明できるかもしれない様々な理論がある。イヤーワームは，「意志によらない記憶（involuntary memory）」と呼ばれる，より大きな現象，それは特定の食べ物についての考えが頭の中に浮かんだあとにそれを食べたくなることや，突然，長い間会っていない友人のことを考えることを含むものだが，その現象の一部であるかもしれない。

重要語句リスト

☐ commonly	副	一般に，普通は
☐ identify	動	明らかにする，発見する
☐ a set of 〜	熟	一連の〜
☐ trigger	名	誘因
☐ cause	動	引き起こす，〜の原因となる
☐ tune	名	曲
☐ pop into one's head	熟	（人の）頭に浮かぶ
☐ stay	動	とどまる，滞在する
☐ common	形	一般の，共通の，ありふれた
☐ recently	副	つい最近，近ごろ
☐ stick	動	（いつまでも）残る，（心から）離れない
☐ repeatedly	副	繰り返して
☐ for a long time	熟	長い間，当分の間
☐ case	名	場合，事件
☐ current	形	現在の
☐ situation	名	状況
☐ memory	名	記憶
☐ cause	名	原因
☐ stress	名	ストレス，重圧
☐ report	名	報告
☐ frequently	副	頻繁に
☐ examination	名	試験
☐ return	動	戻る
☐ at other times	熟	別の機会に
☐ various	形	様々な，色々な
☐ theory	名	理論
☐ explain	動	説明する
☐ include	動	含む
☐ desire	名	願望，欲求
☐ particular	形	特定の
☐ suddenly	副	突然に

❸ There are a couple of reasons <why this might happen (with music)>. One is [that music is (often) recorded (in a very personal and emotional way), and personal or emotional connections are retrieved (better) (from memory)]. Some experts suggest [that music may remain (in our heads) (because it is important (for humans) [to remember information])]. Modern humans have been (around) (for about 200,000 years), but (since written language was invented (only around 5,000 years ago)), people memorized important information (through songs). The combination <of rhythm, rhyme, and melody> make songs easier (to recall) (than words alone.)

❹ (So), (how) can we turn (off) earworms? Some suggest [that just thinking <of another song> will push (out) the first one]. Others suggest [that everyday activities help, (like [going for a run], or [doing a crossword puzzle])]. (In fact), anything <which can distract our brain (from having to "listen" (to the same song) (repeatedly))> may help.

❸ このようなことが音楽に対して起こりうるいくつかの理由がある。1つは，音楽はしばしば，非常に個人的で感情的な方法で記録され，個人的あるいは感情的なつながりは記憶からより良く取り戻されるからである。人間にとって情報を記憶していることは重要であるので，音楽は頭の中に残っているのかもしれないと示す専門家もいる。現生人類は約20万年の間存在しているが，書き言葉はほんの5,000年ほど前に考案されたので，人々は歌を通して重要な情報を記憶した。リズム，韻，メロディーの組み合わせにより，歌詞だけよりも，歌を思い出しやすくなる。

❹ では，どのようにしたらイヤーワームを止めることができるのだろうか。ただ別の曲について考えることが，最初の曲を押し出してくれると示す人がいる。また走ったり，クロスワードパズルに取り組んだりというような毎日の活動が役立つと示す人もいる。実際，同じ曲を繰り返し「聴」かなければならないということから脳をまぎらすことができるものなら何でも役立つのかもしれない。

□ a couple of ~	熟 いくつかの~，2・3(人)の~
□ record	動 記録する
□ personal	形 個人的な
□ emotional	形 感情的な，感情の
□ connection	名 つながり，関係
□ retrieve	動 取り戻す
□ expert	名 専門家
□ suggest	動 示す，提案する
□ remain	動 残る，~のままでいる
□ remember	動 記憶している，思い出す
□ information	名 情報
□ modern humans	名 現生人類
□ invent	動 考案する，発明する
□ memorize	動 記憶する
□ combination	名 組み合わせ
□ rhythm	名 リズム，周期
□ rhyme	名 韻
□ melody	名 メロディー，旋律
□ recall	動 思い出す
□ ~ alone	副 ~だけ
□ turn off ~	熟 ~を止める
□ activity	名 活動
□ crossword	名 クロスワード
□ distract	動 まぎらす，気をそらす

Lesson 04
問題文

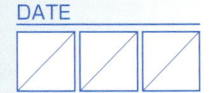

Read the passage and answer the following questions.

Catastrophes can, and do, happen. As humans or as communities and even whole societies, none of us are free from fate.

The irony is that while we may have reached a stage in human development where we have more technology at our disposal than ever before, we have also forgotten many of the skills that our ancestors depended on for their own survival.

Today we take it for granted that we can talk to each other and see each other in an instant on opposite sides of the earth. Apart from the deepest reaches of the oceans, there is virtually nowhere on the planet that is inaccessible.

What happens, however, when modern technology is suddenly, and unexpectedly, taken away? When electricity is cut off, we are suddenly plunged into darkness and silence; our computer and television screens go blank and we are unable to communicate with the rest of the world. Our heating fails and we can't wash or feed ourselves. For a while, for just a few hours, it all seems quite a novelty. We discover we have neighbors and talk to strangers and help each other out: things we don't do as much as we should in normal life. Then suddenly the lights come back on and we all return to business as usual, confident that it was just a temporary situation and we don't need to worry about it happening again for a long time.

Our growing dependence on technologies of all forms is a double-edged sword. The fact that our modern world has, at least (x)<u>on the face of it</u>, become increasingly reliable has, paradoxically, made us weaker and weaker. People are no longer able to cope for more than a very short time when these systems fail.

What happens when the technology on which we depend is entirely taken away, when suddenly we have no means to communicate, or when we find ourselves alone in a strange new world — maybe a desert, a jungle, or a mountain glacier*? How this has come about in the first place is unimportant. Your light plane may have crashed on a short hop over the mountains to a remote lodge. You may have become separated from a trekking party in the mountains, or found yourself in a whiteout* on a mountain trail. To your disbelief, you find yourself with nothing other than the clothes you stand up in. You are lost and alone, maybe presumed dead, and no one is looking for you anymore.

No cell phone or GPS can help you now. They have all been left behind on that faraway planet called civilization. You have no shelter, no water, no fire, and no idea where you are — and evening is falling. There are wild creatures and other dangers all around you and it is beginning to get very cold. What you wouldn't give for seemingly ordinary and low-tech items, such as a lighter or a water bottle, or a sleeping bag to keep you warm. Even a simple toy compass would be nice. But no matter how much you may want them, they all remain locked firmly away in that distant land you have allowed yourself to become so dependent on.

* glacier (氷河)　whiteout (ホワイトアウト〔あたり一面が白く見え，地形の見分けがつかなくなる現象〕)

Lesson 04
設問

(1) What is the main topic of the passage?

1 The growing frequency of natural disasters

2 The risks of people living alone

3 The need to upgrade low-tech items

4 The reliance on various technologies

(2) Which of the following is NOT mentioned as a result of system failure in paragraph 4?

1 Breakdowns in communication

2 Interruptions of heating systems

3 Criminals acting under darkness

4 Difficulties in securing adequate food

(3) The phrase "on the face of it" in line (X) is closest in meaning to

1 By one's cheek

2 At a surface level

3 Without a center

4 Through a pattern

(4) Why does the author mention "wild creatures" in paragraph 7?

1 To exemplify the risks of a situation
2 To show why people should not travel alone
3 To suggest that nature must be protected
4 To outline the excitement of seeing new things

No.	(1)	(2)	(3)	(4)
配点	10点	10点	15点	15点
解答欄				

Lesson 04
解答・解説

（1） 本文の主なトピックは何か。
1 自然災害のさらなる頻発
2 一人暮らしの危険性
3 低科学技術の製品を改良する必要性
④ 様々な科学技術への依存

解説 ▶ 本文は「大災害はおそらく，また，必ず起こるものである」という導入で始まり，続く段落以降では，**大災害＝我々が依存する様々な科学技術が突然失われた場合**について述べられている。よって，**4** が正解だとわかる。

（2） 第4段落のシステム障害の結果として述べられていないものは以下のどれか。
1 コミュニケーションの崩壊
2 暖房装置の停止
③ 暗闇の中で行われる犯罪
4 十分な食料を確保する難しさ

解説 ▶ **1** は第4段落第2文後半「世界のそのほかの人々とコミュニケーションをとることができなくなる」，**2** は第3文前半「暖房装置は停止し」，**4** は第3文後半「食事ができなくなる」でそれぞれ述べられている。よって，**3** が正解となる。

（3） 下線部（X）の「on the face of it」という表現は，……に最も意味が近い。
1 ほおの側で
② 表面レベルで
3 中心なしに
4 パターンを通して

解説 ▶ 慣用表現「on the face of it」は，「表面上は」「一見したところ」という意味。よって，正解は **2** となる。

(4) 第7段落で筆者が「wild creatures」について言及しているのはなぜか。
① ある状況の危険を例証するため
2 なぜ人々が独りで旅行をすべきではないのかを示すため
3 自然が守られなければならないことを示すため
4 新しい物を見ることの興奮を概説するため

解説▶ 本文は全体を通して，**大災害＝我々が依存するさまざまな科学技術が突然失われた場合に起こりうる危険性**について述べている。**1**の「ある状況」とは**科学技術が突然失われた場合**であると予想できる。つまり，wild creatures（野生生物）も，大災害が起こった際に**直面しうる危険**を述べた一例であること考えることができるため，**1**が正解となる。

No.	（1）	（2）	（3）	（4）
配点	10点	10点	15点	15点
解答欄	**4**	**3**	**2**	**1**

正解

得点	（1回目） /50点	（2回目）	（3回目）	CHECK YOUR LEVEL	0〜30点 ➡ *Work harder!* 31〜40点 ➡ *OK!* 41〜50点 ➡ *Way to go!*

47

Lesson 04
構造分析

[　]＝名詞　　□＝修飾される名詞　　＜　＞＝形容詞・同格　　(　)＝副詞
S＝主語　V＝動詞　O＝目的語　C＝補語　'＝従節

❶ Catastrophes can, and do, happen. (As humans) or (as communities and even whole societies), none <of us> are free (from fate).

❷ The irony is [that (while we may have reached a stage <in human development> <where we have more technology (at our disposal) (than ever before)>), we have (also) forgotten many <of the skills <that our ancestors depended on (for their own survival)>>].

❸ Today we take it (for granted) [that we can talk (to each other) and see each other (in an instant) (on opposite sides of the earth)]. (Apart from the deepest reaches <of the oceans>), there is (virtually) nowhere (on the planet) <that is inaccessible>.

❹ What happens, (however), (when modern technology is (suddenly), and (unexpectedly), taken away)? (When electricity is cut (off)), we are (suddenly) plunged (into darkness and silence); our computer and television screens go blank and we are unable to communicate (with the rest <of the world>). Our heating fails and we can't wash or feed ourselves. (For a while), (for just a few hours), it (all) seems (quite) a novelty. We discover [we have neighbors and talk (to strangers) and help each other (out)]: things <we don't do (as much) (as we should (in normal life))>. (Then) (suddenly) the lights come (back) on and we (all) return (to business) (as usual), (confident [that it was (just) a temporary situation and we don't need (to worry (about it happening) (again) (for a long time))]).

48

Lesson 04 (4／5) 問題文→設問→解答・解説→**構造分析**

【和訳】

❶ 大災害はおそらく，また，必ず起こるものである。人間として，あるいは共同体や社会全体としてでさえ，我々は誰も運命から逃れられない。

❷ 皮肉なのは，我々は自由に使える科学技術をかつてなかったほどに有する人類の発展段階に到達したかもしれないけれども，我々はまた，祖先が自身の生存のために頼りにしていた技術の多くを忘れてしまっているということである。

❸ 今日，我々は地球の反対側にいても，即座に，お互いに会話をしたり，お互いを見たりすることができるということを当然のことと思っている。海の最も深い区域を除いて，事実上，（人間が）近づきにくい場所など地球上にはどこにもない。

❹ しかし，現代の科学技術が突然，そして思いがけなく取り除かれたとき，何が起こるだろうか。電力が断ち切られるとき，我々は突然暗闇と沈黙（という状況）に追いやられる。コンピュータやテレビ画面には何も映らなくなり，世界のそのほかの人々とコミュニケーションをとることができなくなる。暖房装置は停止し，身体を洗うことや，食事ができなくなる。しばらく，ほんの数時間，それはすべて非常に新しいことのように思える。ご近所さんがいて，見知らぬ人に話しかけ，お互いに助け合っているということがわかる。それらは普段の生活の中で我々がすべきほどは行っていないことである。その後，突然電力が戻り，我々は皆いつものように業務に戻る。というのも，それは一時的な事態で当分の間はその事態がもう一度起こることを心配する必要はないと確信しているからだ。

重要語句リスト

☐ catastrophe	图 大災害
☐ fate	图 運命
☐ irony	图 皮肉
☐ while S V	接 S が V だけれども
☐ reach	動 到達する，届く
☐ stage	图 段階
☐ at one's disposal	熟（人が）自由に使える
☐ ancestor	图 祖先
☐ depend on ~	熟 ~に頼る，~を当てにする
☐ take it for granted that S V	熟 S が V することを当然のことと思う
☐ in an instant	熟 即座に
☐ opposite	形 反対側の，逆の
☐ apart from ~	熟 ~を除いて，~から切り離して
☐ virtually	副 事実上
☐ nowhere	副 どこにも……ない
☐ inaccessible	形 近づきにくい
☐ unexpectedly	副 思いがけなく
☐ take away ~	熟 ~を取り除く
☐ electricity	图 電力
☐ cut off ~	熟 ~を断ち切る，~を切りとる
☐ plunge A into B	熟 A を B に追いやる
☐ darkness	图 暗闇
☐ silence	图 沈黙
☐ blank	形 何もない，白紙の
☐ be unable to V	熟 V できない
☐ communicate with ~	熟 ~とコミュニケーションをとる，~と連絡を取り合う
☐ heating	图 暖房装置
☐ fail	動 停止する，失敗する
☐ feed	動 食事を与える
☐ for a while	熟 しばらく（の間）
☐ quite	副 非常に，かなり
☐ novelty	图 新しいこと
☐ stranger	图 見知らぬ人，他人
☐ return	動 戻る
☐ business	图 業務，仕事
☐ as usual	熟 いつものように
☐ confident	形 確信している
☐ temporary	形 一時的な
☐ situation	图 事態，状況
☐ for a long time	熟 当分の間，長い間

Lesson 04

49

❺ Our growing dependence on technologies of all forms is a double-edged sword. The fact that our modern world has, (at least) (on the face of it), become (increasingly) reliable has, (paradoxically), made us weaker and weaker. People are (no longer) able to cope (for more than a very short time) (when these systems fail).

❻ What happens (when the technology on which we depend is (entirely) taken away), (when (suddenly) we have no means to communicate), or (when we find ourselves alone (in a strange new world) — maybe a desert, a jungle, or a mountain glacier)? [How this has come (about) (in the first place)] is unimportant. Your light plane may have crashed (on a short hop) (over the mountains) (to a remote lodge). You may have become separated (from a trekking party) (in the mountains), or found yourself (in a whiteout) (on a mountain trail). (To your disbelief), you find yourself (with nothing other than the clothes you stand up in). You are lost and alone, ((maybe) presumed dead), and no one is looking (for you) (anymore).

❼ No cell phone or GPS can help you (now). They have (all) been left (behind) (on that faraway planet called civilization). You have no shelter, no water, no fire, and no idea where you are — and evening is falling. There are wild creatures and other dangers (all around you) and it is beginning to get very cold. What you wouldn't give (for seemingly ordinary and low-tech items, such as a lighter or a water bottle, or a sleeping bag to keep you warm). (Even) a simple toy compass would be nice. But ((no matter how much) you may want them), they (all) remain locked (firmly) (away) (in that distant land you have allowed yourself (to become so dependent on)).

Lesson 04 (5／5) 問題文→設問→解答・解説→**構造分析**

❺ あらゆる形態における科学技術への依存の高まりは諸刃の剣である。現代社会が，少なくとも表面上は，ますます信頼できるものになっているという事実が，逆説的だが，我々人間をますます弱くしているのだ。このようなシステムが停止するとき，人間はほんの短い時間でさえ，もはや乗り切ることができない。

❻ 我々が依存している科学技術が完全に取り払われたとき，突然コミュニケーションをとる手段がなくなったとき，また，砂漠やジャングル，山岳氷河のようななじみがない新しい世界で自分1人だとわかったとき，何が起こるだろうか。そもそも，このようなことがどのように生じるかは重要ではない。乗っていた軽飛行機が，山を越えて遠くの山小屋へ向かう短距離飛行の途中で墜落してしまうかもしれない。山の中でトレッキングの集団からはぐれてしまうかもしれないし，山道でホワイトアウトしたと気づくかもしれない。信じられないことに，着ている服以外に何も自分が身につけていないことに気づくのである。道に迷い1人になり，おそらく死んだと推定され，もはや誰もあなたを探していない。

❼ 携帯電話やGPSも今は当てにならない。それらはすべて文明と呼ばれる遠い惑星においてきてしまった。（避難する）小屋も，水も，火もなく，自分がどこにいるのか見当もつかず，日が暮れていく。周りには野生生物やそのほかの危険がつきまとい，非常に寒くなり始める。ライターや水筒，暖をとるための寝袋のような，一見ありふれた，低科学技術のものを得るためになんでもするだろう。簡単なおもちゃの方位磁石でさえ良いだろう。しかし，どれほどそれらを欲しても，それらはあなたが非常に依存するようになってしまった遠い世界に，すべてしっかりと閉じ込められたままである。

□ grow	動 増加する
□ dependence on ~	熟 ~への依存
□ form	名 形態
□ double-edged sword	名 諸刃の剣
□ at least	熟 少なくとも
□ on the face of it	熟 表面上は
□ increasingly	副 ますます
□ reliable	形 信頼できる
□ paradoxically	副 逆説的に
□ 比較級 and 比較級	熟 ますます…
□ no longer	熟 もはや……でない
□ be able to V	熟 Vできる
□ cope	動 乗り切る，対処する
□ system	名 システム，体制
□ entirely	副 完全に
□ means	名 手段，方法
□ desert	名 砂漠
□ jungle	名 ジャングル
□ in the first place	熟 そもそも
□ unimportant	形 重要でない
□ may have Vpp	熟 Vだったかもしれない
□ crash	動 墜落する
□ hop	名 飛行
□ remote	形 遠い，遠く離れた
□ lodge	名 山小屋
□ separated	形 はぐれた，離ればなれの
□ trek	動 トレッキングする，徒歩旅行する
□ trail	名 小道
□ disbelief	名 信じられないこと
□ presume	動 推定する
□ faraway	形 遠い
□ civilization	名 文明，文化
□ shelter	名 小屋，隠れ場
□ creature	名 生物
□ seemingly	副 一見，うわべは
□ ordinary	形 ありふれた，一般の
□ remain	動 ~のままである，残る
□ firmly	副 しっかりと

END

Read the passage and answer the following questions.

　Kids are usually far better than adults at learning how to speak multiple languages. A new study suggests that babies between 4 and 6 months old can tell the difference between two languages just by looking at the speaker's face. They don't need to hear a word. Sometime between 6 and 8 months of age, babies raised in homes where just one language is spoken lose this ability. On the other hand, babies from bilingual homes keep the face-reading ability until they're at least 8 months old.

　Researchers in Canada, at the University of British Columbia in Vancouver, studied 36 infants from English-speaking families. Twelve of the babies were 4 months old, 12 were 6 months old, and the rest were 8 months old. Each baby sat on his or her mother's lap and watched video clips of a woman talking. The woman was fluent in both English and French. In some clips, she read from a storybook in English. In other clips, she read in French. In all of the videos, there was no sound.

　After watching clip after clip of the woman reading in just one language, the babies eventually started to look away, apparently because they were bored. The researchers then showed the babies a new silent clip of the woman reading a story in the other language. At that point, the 4- and 6-month olds started looking at the screen again. The 8-month olds, by contrast, paid no attention.

The second study involved a different set of 36 infants of the same ages. These babies were from English-speaking homes. They watched silent clips of the woman reading one set of sentences in either English or French until they grew bored. Then, they saw clips showing the woman read different sentences, but in the same language that she had already been speaking. None of the babies showed a renewed interest.

　　A third trial included 24 infants of the same ages whose families spoke both English and French at home. In the first set of clips, the woman spoke in one language, and in the second set she used the other language. All babies in this study looked longer at clips after the woman switched languages. That suggests that, in bilingual families, a baby's ability to distinguish between languages continues at least until eight months of age.

　　Together, these results suggest that "visual information about speech may play a more critical role in language learning than previously expected," says leading researcher and psychologist Whitney M. Weikum. It's not yet clear, she adds, which part of the speaker's face babies are looking at for clues.

　　Next, scientists want to see whether babies can match faces with the voices of foreign-language speakers. If babies can do this, the scientists would then like to know if this ability also declines toward the end of the first year of life.

Lesson 05
設問

(1) According to paragraph 1, what are 4-month-old babies able to do?

    1 Connect a speaker's facial activity to language changes

    2 Understand which adults are bilingual and which are not

    3 Say words that they have not even heard from adults yet

    4 Express their ideas mainly through facial expressions

(2) Which of the following study results is described in paragraph 3?

    1 Babies reacted based on their age.

    2 Older babies were smarter than younger ones.

    3 Audio clips generated more interest than silent clips.

    4 New speakers gained more attention than familiar ones.

(3) In paragraphs 3 and 4, the author's primary purpose is to

    1 suggest that an earlier study was wrong.

    2 indicate that two studies should be combined.

    3 illustrate different outcomes from different tests.

    4 propose reasons why a new study was accurate.

(4) What paragraph topic most likely follows this passage?

    1 Matching language to education level

    2 Comparing language fluency among children

    3 Understanding the second year of babies' lives

    4 Identifying foreign-language speakers by voice

No.	(1)	(2)	(3)	(4)
配点	10点	10点	15点	15点
解答欄				

解 答 用 紙

Lesson 05
解答・解説

(1) 第1段落によると，生後4ヵ月の乳児にできることは何か。
  ① 話す人の顔の動きを言語の変化に結び付ける（顔の動きから言語の違いを区別する）
  ② どの大人が2言語使用で，どの大人が2言語使用でないかを理解する
  ③ まだ大人から聞いたことのない言葉を言う
  ④ 主に表情を通して，自分たちの考えを表現する

解説 ▶ 第1段落第2文「あらたな研究は，生後4ヵ月から6ヵ月の乳児は話す人の顔を見るだけで，2つの言語の違いを見分けることができると示している」より，**1**が正解とわかる。

(2) 以下の研究結果のうちどれが第3段落で述べられているか。
  ① 乳児は月齢に応じた反応をした。
  ② より生まれの早い乳児の方が，より生まれの遅い乳児よりも賢かった。
  ③ 音声クリップの方が，無音クリップよりも興味を引き起こした。
  ④ 新顔の話者の方が，顔なじみの話者よりも注意を引いた。

解説 ▶ 第1段落より，本文は「生後4ヵ月から6ヵ月の乳児は話す人の顔を見るだけで，2つの言語の違いを見分けることができる」という研究について述べられていると判断できる。これをふまえ，第3段落では，ある言語の無声ビデオを見飽きたあとに，それとは別の言葉の無声ビデオを見たとき，生後4ヵ月から6ヵ月の乳児は興味を示したが，8ヵ月の乳児は興味を示さなかったという実験結果が述べられているので，この実験結果の趣旨は，**生後4ヵ月から6ヵ月の乳児は話し手の顔と言語の変化に気がついたが，8ヵ月の乳児は気がつかなかった**ということであるとわかる。よって，**1**が正解となる。

(3) 第3段落と第4段落において，著者の主要な目的は……ことだ。
1 より早い時期に行われた研究は間違っていたということを示す
2 2つの研究は同時に行われるべきだということを示す
③ 異なる試験から得られた異なる結果を例証する
4 新しい研究が正確であった理由を提示する

解説▶第3段落では**別の言語で同じ物語**を読んだときの乳児の反応について研究した内容であったが，第4段落では**同じ言語で別の物語**を読んだときの反応について述べられている。よって，**3**が正解となる。

(4) この文章に最も続きそうな段落トピックは何か。
1 言語を教育レベルに合わせること
2 子供たちの言語の流暢さを比較すること
③ 2年目の幼児の生活を理解すること
4 声によって外国語話者を特定すること

解説▶最終段落最終文「科学者たちは，この能力も同様に1歳を迎える頃には衰えていくのかどうかも知りたいと思っている」より，本文に続きそうなトピックは，1歳時の研究＝生後2年目の乳児の研究であることが読み取れる。よって，**3**が正解とわかる。

	正　解			
No.	(1)	(2)	(3)	(4)
配点	10点	10点	15点	15点
解答欄	1	1	3	3

| 得点 | (1回目) /50点 | (2回目) | (3回目) | CHECK YOUR LEVEL | 0～30点 ➡ *Work harder!*
31～40点 ➡ *OK!*
41～50点 ➡ *Way to go!* |

Lesson 05
構造分析

[ ]＝名詞　　□＝修飾される名詞　　< >＝形容詞・同格　　( )＝副詞
S＝主語　V＝動詞　O＝目的語　C＝補語　'＝従節

❶ Kids are (usually) far better (than adults) (at learning [how to speak multiple languages]). A new study suggests [that babies <between 4 and 6 months old> can tell the difference <between two languages> (just) (by looking (at the speaker's face))]. They do(n't) need to hear a word. (Sometime) (between 6 and 8 months of age), babies <raised (in homes <where just one language is spoken>>) lose this ability. (On the other hand), babies <from bilingual homes> keep the face-reading ability (until they're (at least) 8 months old).

❷ Researchers <in Canada>, <at the University of British Columbia in Vancouver>, studied 36 infants <from English-speaking families>. Twelve <of the babies> were 4 months old, 12 were 6 months old, and the rest were 8 months old. Each baby sat (on his or her mother's lap) and watched video clips <of a woman talking>. The woman was fluent (in both English and French). (In some clips), she read (from a storybook) (in English). (In other clips), she read (in French). (In all <of the videos>), there was no sound.

❸ (After watching clip (after clip) <of the woman reading (in just one language)>), the babies (eventually) started to look (away), (apparently) (because they were bored). The researchers (then) showed the babies a new silent clip <of the woman <reading a story (in the other language)>>. (At that point), the 4- and 6- month olds started looking (at the screen) (again). The 8-month olds, (by contrast), paid no attention.

【和訳】

❶ 子供はたいてい，大人よりもはるかに，複数の言語の話し方を学ぶのが得意である。あらたな研究は，生後4ヵ月から6ヵ月の乳児は話す人の顔を見るだけで，2つの言語の違いを見分けることができると示している。彼らは単語を聞く必要がないのだ。生後6ヵ月から8ヵ月の間のあるときに，たった1つの言語しか話されない家庭で育てられた乳児はこの能力を失う。一方で，2言語を使用する家庭で育った乳児は，少なくとも8ヵ月になるまでは（話者の）顔から（言語の違いを）読み取る能力を保持している。

❷ カナダの研究者たちは，バンクーバーにあるブリティッシュ・コロンビア大学で，英語を話す家族の乳児36人を調査した。そのうち12人は生後4ヵ月，また別の12人は6ヵ月，残りは8ヵ月であった。それぞれの乳児は母親のひざの上に座り，ある女性が話しているビデオクリップを見た。その女性は英語とフランス語の両方が流暢であった。あるビデオクリップでは，彼女は物語の本の一部を英語で読んだ。また別のビデオクリップでは，彼女はフランス語で読んだ。すべてのビデオにおいて，音はなかった。

❸ 1つの言語だけで（話を）読み進める女性のビデオクリップを次々見ると，乳児は明らかに退屈し，最終的に目をそらし始めた。それから，研究者たちは，乳児に，もう1つの言語で物語を読んでいる女性のあらたな無声のビデオクリップを見せた。そのとき，生後4ヵ月と6ヵ月の乳児は再び画面を見始めた。対照的に，8ヵ月の乳児は何の注意も払わなかった。

重要語句リスト

multiple	複数の
tell the difference between A and B	AとBの違いを見分ける
look at ~	~を見る
need to V	Vする必要がある
raise	育てる，上げる
ability	能力，機能
on the other hand	一方で
bilingual	2言語使用の，2カ国語を話す
at least ~	少なくとも~
researcher	研究者，調査員
infant	幼児
rest	残り，休憩
each	それぞれの
sit on ~	~に座る
lap	ひざ
video clip	ビデオクリップ
fluent	流暢な
both A and B	AもBも両方とも
storybook	物語の本，童話の本
sound	音
eventually	結局は，ついに
look away	目をそらす
apparently	明らかに，どうやら~らしい
bored	退屈した
silent	無声の，静かな
by contrast	対照的に
pay attention (to ~)	(~に) 注意を払う

❹ The second study involved a different set <of 36 infants> <of the same ages>>. These babies were (from English-speaking homes). They watched silent clips <of the woman> <reading one set> <of sentences (in either English or French)>>> (until they grew bored). (Then), they saw clips <showing [the woman read different sentences]>, but (in the same language <that she had (already) been speaking>). None <of the babies> showed a renewed interest.

❺ A third trial included 24 infants <of the same ages> <whose families spoke both English and French (at home)>. (In the first set of clips), the woman spoke (in one language), and (in the second set) she used the other language. All babies <in this study> looked (longer) (at clips) (after the woman switched languages). That suggests [that, (in bilingual families), a baby's ability <to distinguish between languages> continues (at least) (until eight months of age)].

❻ (Together), these results suggest [that "visual information <about speech> may play a more critical role (in language learning) (than previously expected)]," says leading researcher and psychologist Whitney M. Weikum. It's not (yet) clear, {she adds}, [which part of the speaker's face <babies are looking at (for clues)>].

❼ (Next), scientists want to see [whether babies can match faces (with the voices <of foreign-language speakers>)]. (If babies can do this), the scientists would (then) like to know [if this ability (also) declines (toward the end <of the first year of life>)].

❹ 第2の研究は，第1の研究とは異なる，同じ年齢36人の乳児に関するものであった。これらの乳児は英語を話す家庭で育った。彼らは退屈するまで，英語かフランス語かどちらかの文を読んでいる女性の無声のビデオクリップを見た。それから，彼らは，その女性が異なる文を読んでいるのを示すビデオクリップを見たが，（それは）彼女がすでに話してきていたのと同じ言語であった。どの乳児も興味を取り戻すことはなかった。

❺ 第3の試みは，家族が家で英語とフランス語の両方を話す同年齢の24人の幼児に関するものであった。最初のビデオクリップの場面では，女性は1つの言語を話し，その次の場面で彼女はもう1つの言語を使った。この研究に参加したすべての乳児は，女性が言語を変えたあと，ビデオクリップをより長く見た。それは，2言語を使用している家庭では，言語を区別する乳児の能力は少なくとも8ヵ月までは続くということを示している。

❻ 全体として，これらの結果は，「話し方に関する視覚的な情報は，以前考えられていた以上に，言語学習においてより重要な役割を果たしているかもしれない」と，先導する研究者で心理学者のWhitney M. Weikumは述べた。彼女は，乳児が手がかりとして見ているのが話す人の顔のどの部分なのかはまだ明確ではないと付け加えた。

❼ 次に，科学者たちは，乳児が顔とその外国語を話す人の声を一致させることができるのかどうかを調べたいと思っている。もし乳児がこうすることができるのなら，そうすれば科学者たちは，この能力も同様に1歳を迎える頃には衰えていくのかどうかも知りたいと思っている。

☐ involve	動	含む，巻き込む
☐ a set of 〜	熟	一連の〜
☐ sentence	名	文，文章
☐ either A or B	熟	AかBのどちらか
☐ already	副	すでに
☐ renewed interest		よみがえった興味，新しい関心
☐ trial	名	試み，試験
☐ switch	動	変更する，切り替える
☐ distinguish	動	区別する，識別する
☐ continue	動	続く
☐ together	副	全体として
☐ visual	形	視覚の
☐ speech	名	話し方，演説
☐ critical	形	重要な
☐ role	名	役割
☐ previously	副	以前は
☐ expect		考える，予期する
☐ psychologist	名	心理学者
☐ add	動	付け加える
☐ part of 〜	熟	〜の一部
☐ clue	名	手がかり，道しるべ，証拠
☐ whether S V	接	SがVするかどうか
☐ match	動	一致させる
☐ would like to V	熟	Vしたい
☐ decline	動	衰える，断る
☐ toward	前	〜のほうへ向かって

Special Column（生徒から東進講師陣に質問！）

Please teach me, teacher!

Q 「英語4技能」って何ですか？
なんで英語4技能が必要なんですか？

A 英語における4技能とは，Listening（リスニング【聞く】）・Speaking（スピーキング【話す】）・Reading（リーディング【読む】）・Writing（ライティング【書く】）の4つを指します。

　英語4技能が必要とされている理由はいくつかありますが，私が最も重要視しているのは日本という国が置かれている状況にあります。現況が続けば，少子高齢化は加速し，そう遠くない未来において人口減が約束されてしまっている国，それが日本です。そうなれば，国内で流通する貨幣の絶対量が減少し，経済は乏しくなる。経済が乏しくなれば，税収も減少する。税収が減少すれば，社会保障はもちろん，公共事業などを通じて先進的なものを導入することも困難になる。極論を言えば，「発展途上国」となる可能性さえ否定しきれない。それがこの国の抱えた現状であると言えます。当然ですが，我々はそのような状況を回避すべく，行動しなければなりません。その行動の1つが，英語4技能の習得だと私は思っています。

　英語4技能を習得すれば，英語という共通言語を介し，様々な国々とつながることが可能です。時には自らが海外へ出向き，時には海外の顧客を日本に招き入れ，まさに世界を舞台に活躍することができるようになります。結果として，日本に流通する貨幣の絶対量も増え，経済の活性化にも貢献することは間違いないでしょう。もちろん，英語4技能を習得するだけで，すべてがうまく動き出すことはありません。ただ，すべてをうまく動かすカギの1つが「英語」であるというのも事実です。日本の未来を担う皆さんが，大学受験レベルの英語力を目標とするのではなく，まずは，その先を見据えた英語力，すなわち「英語4技能」を身につける。さらに，進学先では，世界で勝負できる専門性の高い知識を身につける。ここから，新しい日本が始まるのだと私は確信しています。

（回答：東進英語科講師）

Premium Reading Workbook

Standard
STAGE-2

Lesson 06–10

Columbia University is one of the world's most important centers of research and at the same time a distinctive and distinguished learning environment for undergraduates and graduate students in many scholarly and professional fields. The University recognizes the importance of its location in New York City and seeks to link its research and teaching to the vast resources of a great metropolis. It seeks to attract a diverse and international faculty and student body, to support research and teaching on global issues, and to create academic relationships with many countries and regions.

Columbia University

Lesson 06
問題文

単語数 ▶ 443 words
制限時間 ▶ 20 分
目標得点 ▶ 40 / 50点

DATE

■ Read the passage and answer the following questions.

Romantic heartbreak hurts. (1)? Researchers now have a better understanding of this problem. New research shows that the same regions of the brain that are activated when people experience pain in their bodies also become active when people feel rejected by someone they love.

The findings suggest that people whose feelings are crushed in a romantic breakup also may feel actual physical pain, says University of Michigan social psychologist Ethan Kross, lead author of the study reported Monday in the *Proceedings of the National Academy of Sciences*.

Kross, an assistant professor in the psychology department, teamed with his colleagues and researchers at Columbia University and the University of Colorado-Boulder to recruit 40 people who had gone through a romantic breakup during the past six months. All said their breakups (2) intense feelings of rejection and pain.

Participants underwent functional* magnetic resonance imaging (fMRI) scans while they viewed photos of their ex-partner* and thought about how they felt during their breakup. They also had fMRI scans while they viewed a photo of a friend and thought about a recent positive experience with that person. Finally, they received fMRI scans while they wore an arm device that created bearable pains to measure physical pain reactions.

Researchers compared the findings with 500 scans of other people's brain responses to physical pain, emotion and other psychological processes.

"We found that the intense experience of social rejection activates regions of the brain that are involved in the sensory* experience of physical pain," Kross says.

The study builds on previous research that shows both rejection and physical pain activate another set of brain regions involved in negative emotions. "The mind, brain and body are (3)," Kross says. "These findings may offer insights into how heartbreak and rejection can lead to different types of physical illness and disorders."

Mark Leary, a professor of psychology and neuroscience* at Duke University who has studied hurt feelings, says the connection between pain and heartbreak makes sense: "We're motivated to maintain good relationships and try to repair them when problems arise because breakups and rejections hurt. It's a way of keeping us adjusted to the quality of our relationships." Naomi Eisenberger, an assistant professor of psychology at UCLA, says her research shows that taking Tylenol, a physical pain reliever*, diminished the pain of hurt feelings and social exclusion.

She hasn't studied its use for the intense feelings of heartbreak, but she says the latest research "continues to highlight the fact that humans are an extraordinarily (4) species — so much so that social rejection is interpreted by the brain as being as harmful as damage to the (5) body."

(Nanci Hellmich, USA TODAY, 2011.3.29, slightly modified)

* functional magnetic resonance imaging (fMRI)
（機能的磁気共鳴画像装置〔脳内の活動部位を画像化する際に使用される装置〕）
ex-partner（かつての恋人）　　sensory（感覚〔上〕の）
neuroscience（神経科学）　　reliever（緩和剤）

Lesson 06
設問

Choose the best word or phrase from among the four choices to fill each gap.

(1) 1 And if   2 So what
     3 But why   4 Why not

(2) 1 led to   2 fell over
     3 stopped from   4 kept out of

(3) 1 severely twisted   2 tightly linked
     3 jointly recognized 4 negatively combined

(4) 1 debatable   2 influential
     3 social   4 mobile

(5) 1 spiritual   2 unlimited
     3 educated   4 physical

解 答 用 紙

No.	(1)	(2)	(3)	(4)	(5)
配点	10点	10点	10点	10点	10点
解答欄					

Lesson 06
解答・解説

(1) 1 そして,もしそうであれば　　2 それがどうしたか
　　3 しかし,それはなぜだろうか　　4 なぜそうしないのだろうか

解説▶ 空所前で「失恋は苦痛を伴う」と述べ,空所後では「現在の研究者はこの問題についてより良く理解をしている」と続け,このあとはその理解している内容を説明し,「失恋は苦痛を伴う」という考えを裏付けている。よって,**3**が正解とわかる。

(2) **1 ～につながった**　　2 落ちた
　　3 ～から止まった　　4 ～に近づかなかった

解説▶ 「全員が,自身の破局は激しい拒否感と苦痛（ 2 ）と述べた」が文意。第4～5段落では,Kross氏らが行った,破局による心の痛みと身体的な痛みとの関連を裏付ける実験について述べられている。第6段落では,実験結果をふまえ「我々は,社会的に拒否される強烈な経験は,身体的な痛みを感覚的に経験する際に関係する脳の領域を活性化させると発見した」より,**自身の破局による心の痛みが,身体的な痛みへとつながる**ことが読み取れる。よって,「原因 lead to 結果」の関係を導く**1**が正解とわかる。

(3) 1 激しく巻き付けられた　　**2 きつく結び付けられている**
　　3 共に認められている　　4 悪い方に組み合わせられている

解説▶ 「心,脳,そして体は（ 3 ）」が文意。同段落第1文「この研究は,拒否されることと身体的痛みの両方が,後ろ向きの感情に関係する脳のほかの領域を活性化することを示した先の研究をもとにしている」より,「**拒否されること＝心**」「**身体的痛み＝体**」「**後ろ向きの感情に関係する脳のほかの領域＝脳**」の結び付きを述べた段落であることがわかる。よって,**2**が正解と判断できる。

(4) 1 議論の余地のある　　　　2 影響を及ぼす
　　 ③ 社会的な　　　　　　　　4 可動性の

解説▶ ダッシュ（—）には補足説明を加える働きがある。よってダッシュ以降を手がかりにすると「人間は並外れて（ 4 ）種で，非常にそのようで（（ 4 ）種で）あるので**社会的に拒否されることは……有害なものとして脳に解釈される**」から，人間は社会的に認められることを好む種，すなわち**社会的な種**であると判断できる。よって，**3** が正解となる。

(5) 1 精神的な　　　　　　　　2 無制限の
　　 3 教養のある　　　　　　　④ 身体の

解説▶ 本文は，全体を通して「心・体・脳」の結び付きについて述べた文章である。よって，「社会的に拒否されること（＝心）は，（ 5 ）体（＝体）に対する損傷と同じくらい有害なものとして脳（＝脳）に解釈される」の関係になることが予想される。よって，**4** が正解とわかる。

正　解					
No.	(1)	(2)	(3)	(4)	(5)
配点	10点	10点	10点	10点	10点
解答欄	**3**	**1**	**2**	**3**	**4**

| 得点 | （1回目） /50点 | （2回目） | （3回目） | CHECK YOUR LEVEL | 0〜30点 ➡ *Work harder!*
31〜40点 ➡ *OK!*
41〜50点 ➡ *Way to go!* |

Lesson 06
構造分析

[　]=名詞　　□=修飾される名詞　＜　＞=形容詞・同格　（　）=副詞
S=主語　V=動詞　O=目的語　C=補語　′=従節

❶ Romantic heartbreak hurts. But (why)? Researchers <now> have a better understanding <of this problem>. New research shows [that the same regions <of the brain> <that are activated (when people experience pain (in their bodies))> (also) become active (when people feel rejected (by someone <they love>))].

❷ The findings suggest [that people <whose feelings are crushed (in a romantic breakup)> (also) may feel actual physical pain], says University of Michigan social psychologist Ethan Kross, <lead author <of the study <reported Monday (in the *Proceedings of the National Academy of Sciences*)>>>.

❸ Kross, an assistant professor <in the psychology department>, teamed (with his colleagues and researchers <at Columbia University and the University of Colorado-Boulder> (to recruit 40 people <who had gone (through a romantic breakup) (during the past six months)>). All said [their breakups led (to intense feelings <of rejection and pain>)].

❹ Participants underwent functional magnetic resonance imaging (fMRI) scans (while they viewed photos <of their ex-partner> and thought (about [how they felt (during their breakup)])). They (also) had fMRI scans (while they viewed a photo <of a friend> and thought (about a recent positive experience <with that person>). (Finally,) they received fMRI scans (while they wore an arm device <that created bearable pains> (to measure physical pain reactions)).

❺ Researchers compared the findings (with 500 scans <of other people's brain responses> <to physical pain, emotion and other psychological processes>>).

【和訳】

❶ 失恋は苦痛を伴う。しかし，それはなぜだろうか。現在の研究者はこの問題についてより良く理解をしている。新しい研究は，人が身体的な苦痛を経験するときに活発になるのと同じ脳内の領域が，愛する人に拒否されたと感じるときにもまた活発になると示している。

❷ その研究結果は，破局して心が粉々になっている人は実際に身体的な痛みも感じているかもしれないと示していると，ミシガン大学の社会心理学者で，「米国科学アカデミー記要」に月曜日に寄稿された研究論文の主要著者である Ethan Kross は述べている。

❸ Kross 氏，彼は心理学部の助教授であるのだが，彼は，彼の同僚と，コロンビア大学とコロラド大学ボルダー校の研究者たちとチームを組んで，過去6カ月の間に失恋を経験してきた40名を集めた。(失恋を経験した) 全員が，自身の破局は激しい拒否感と苦痛につながったと述べた。

❹ 被験者はかつての恋人の写真を見て，破局のときにどう感じたかについて考えながら機能的磁気共鳴画像装置 (fMRI) の検査を受けた。また彼らは友人の写真を見て，その人との最近の前向きな経験について考えながら，fMRI 検査を受けた。最後に，肉体的な痛みの反応を測るため，我慢できる程度の痛みを作り出す装置を腕に付けて，彼らは fMRI 検査を受けた。

❺ 研究者たちはその結果を，身体的苦痛，感情そしてそのほかの心理過程に対するほかの人々の脳の反応についての500例の検査 (結果) と比較した。

重要語句リスト

romantic	形 恋愛に関する，ロマンチックな
heartbreak	名 傷心
hurt	動 傷つける，痛む
researcher	名 研究者，調査員
understanding	名 理解
region	名 領域，地域
activate	動 活性化する
pain	名 苦痛，痛み
active	形 活発な
reject	動 拒否する，拒絶する
suggest	動 示す，提案する
crush	動 粉々になる，押しつぶす
breakup	名 破局
actual	形 実際の
physical	形 身体の，物理的な
psychologist	名 心理学者
author	名 著者，作家
report	動 発表する，報告する
assistant professor	名 助教授
psychology	名 心理学
department	名 部門，部，学科
team with ~	熟 ~とチームを組む，~と協力する
colleague	名 同僚
recruit	動 集める，募集する
lead to ~	熟 ~につながる，~へと至る
intense	形 激しい，猛烈な
rejection	名 拒否(感)，拒絶
undergo	動 受ける
scan	名 検査
view	動 見る
receive	動 受ける，受け取る
device	名 装置
create	動 創造する
bearable	形 我慢できる
measure	動 計測する，測定する
compare A with B	熟 AをBと比較する
emotion	名 感情
process	名 過程

❻ "We found [that the intense experience <of social rejection> activates regions <of the brain> <that are involved (in the sensory experience <of physical pain)>>]," Kross says.

❼ The study builds (on previous research <that shows [both rejection and physical pain activate another set of brain regions <involved (in negative emotions)>]>). "The mind, brain and body are (tightly) linked," Kross says. "These findings may offer insights (into [how heartbreak and rejection can lead (to different types <of physical illness and disorders>)]])."

❽ Mark Leary, a professor <of psychology and neuroscience> <at Duke University> <who has studied hurt feelings>, says [the connection <between pain and heartbreak> makes sense]: "We're motivated (to maintain good relationships and try to repair them (when problems arise) (because breakups and rejections hurt)). It's a way <of keeping us adjusted (to the quality of our relationships)>." Naomi Eisenberger, <an assistant professor <of psychology> <at UCLA>>, says [her research shows [that taking Tylenol, <a physical pain reliever>, diminished the pain <of hurt feelings and social exclusion>]].

❾ She has(n't) studied its use (for the intense feelings <of heartbreak>), but she says [the latest research "continues to highlight the fact <that humans are an extraordinarily social species> — (so much) (so that social rejection is interpreted (by the brain) (as being <as harmful (as damage (to the physical body))>))]."

❻「我々は，社会的に拒否される強烈な経験は，身体的な痛みを感覚的に経験する際に関係する脳の領域を活性化させると発見した。」とKross氏は述べている。

❼ この研究は，拒否されることと身体的痛みの両方が，後ろ向きの感情に関係する脳のほかの領域を活性化することを示した先の研究をもとにしている。「心，脳，そして体はきつく結び付いている」とKross氏は述べている。「これらの発見は，失恋と拒否されることが様々な種類の身体的な病気や不調にどのようにつながるのかに関する見識を与えてくれるかもしれない。」

❽ Mark Leary氏は，傷ついた感情について研究をしてきたデューク大学の心理学と神経科学の教授であり，（彼は）痛みと失恋の結び付きは道理にかなっていると述べている。「失恋や拒否されることは苦痛を伴うので，問題が起きたとき，私たちは良い関係を保ち，関係を修復しようと試みる。それは，私たちが（他者との）関係の質に順応し続ける方法なのだ。」 Naomi Eisenberger氏は，UCLAの心理学助教授であり，彼女の研究は，タイレノール，これは身体の鎮痛緩和剤であるのだが，これを飲むことが，傷ついた感情や社会的に除外されたという苦痛を減少させると示したと述べている。

❾ 彼女は，失恋という激しい感情へのその（タイレノールの）効用を研究していないが，彼女は最新の研究は「人間は並外れて社会的な種で，非常にそのようで（社会的な種で）あるので社会的に拒否されることは身体に対する損傷と同じくらい有害なものとして脳に解釈されるという事実を強調し続けている」と述べている。

□ be involved in ～	熟 ～に関係している
□ previous	形 以前の
□ tightly	副 きつく，しっかりと
□ link	動 結び付ける，接続する
□ offer	動 与える，提案する
□ insight	名 見識
□ illness	名 病気
□ disorder	名 不調，混乱
□ connection	名 結び付き，関係
□ motivate ～ to V	熟 ～にVする気にさせる
□ maintain	動 保つ，維持する
□ relationship	名 関係，結び付き
□ try to V	熟 Vしようと試みる
□ repair	動 修復する
□ arise	動 起こる，生じる
□ adjust	動 順応させる
□ quality	名 （品）質
□ diminish	動 減少させる
□ exclusion	名 除外
□ latest	形 最新の
□ highlight	動 強調する
□ extraordinarily	副 非常に
□ species	名 種
□ interpret	動 解釈する
□ harmful	形 有害な
□ damage	名 損傷，損害

END

Lesson 07
問題文

■ **Read the passage and answer the following questions.**

　The perception of pain is so fundamental to our survival that it affects our brains in profound ways. There is not one single pain center; (1), the whole brain lights up like a Christmas tree when pain is perceived. In the short term we are immediately prompted to protect the painful area, to remove it from the source of the pain and often to cease all use of the affected area while we examine it. In the longer term, our subconscious behavior is altered. If we hit our head on a specific low beam or handle, next time we'll duck. An experience of pain that lasts for long, continuous periods may affect our emotions and attitudes. We may develop depression and become (2). Alternatively, a severe experience of pain and a conscious awareness of exactly what led to that pain may result in the development of an aversion to anything resembling the cause. We call that aversion fear. The aversion may become a long-term subconscious memory that lasts far longer than your memory of the event that caused it. You may no longer remember the time you fell off the high wall and painfully twisted your ankle as a child, but your fear of heights (3) with you.

　We don't always perceive pain. Even when the nerve cells are sending us pain signals, there are times when it is more important for us simply to run away, rather than roll about on the ground in agony. So there are regions of the brain that actively inhibit our perception of pain, sometimes for just a few minutes, sometimes for several days. (4) there are also areas of the brain that do the reverse, and make us hypersensitive to pain.　When we're safe and recovering, such heightened sensations might, for example, encourage us to avoid using the painful part while it heals.

　　Astonishingly, there used to be considerable confusion about when we first start experiencing pain.　A hundred years ago it was widely accepted that newborn babies simply did not perceive pain at all, because their brains had not developed sufficiently.　Perhaps rather cruelly by today's standards, for decades many 'pin-prick' experiments were conducted on sleeping infants in attempts to understand the onset of pain perception.　Much confusion was caused in those early experiments by the seeming lack of sensitivity of babies straight after birth, which turned out to be because the mothers had received anesthetics while giving birth, and the babies received a small dose via their umbilical cords. Today (as anyone with children can affirm), it is well understood that a baby in pain will show clear (5). Crying, wriggling, fisting, large muscle movements, accompanied by clear respiratory and hormonal changes and erratic sleep, are all clear signs of pain.　But those early scientifically flawed experiments sadly resulted in a culture that disregarded the pain of babies for much too long, despite the true scientific findings.

(Adapted from Peter J. Bentley, The Undercover Scientist, 2009.)

Lesson 07
設問

Choose the best word or phrase from among the four choices to fill each gap.

(1) 1 for example   2 though
     3 instead   4 as such

(2) 1 fewer activities   2 less actively
     3 less active   4 no activation

(3) 1 might select   2 should come
     3 may still be   4 can do

(4) 1 Not only   2 In some respects
     3 Otherwise   4 But

(5) 1 wreckage   2 discomfort
     3 erasure   4 inability

No.	(1)	(2)	(3)	(4)	(5)
配点	10点	10点	10点	10点	10点
解答欄					

解 答 用 紙

Lesson 07
解答・解説

(1) **1** 例えば   **2** けれど（文頭不可）
   ③ その代わりに   **4** そういうものとして

   解説▶「痛みを感じる中枢は1つではなく，（ 1 ）痛みを感じると脳全体がクリスマスツリーのように点灯する」が文意。空所以降では「痛みを感じる中枢は1つではない」とする情報が提示されていることが読み取れる。よって，**3** が正解となる。セミコロン「A（文）；B（文）」はAとBの情報の重さが同じ場合に使用される。**1** の「A（文）．For example B（文）」は，BはAのサポート情報にすぎず，情報の重さは「A＞B」の関係になるため，ここでは不可。また，**2** は文中・文尾で使用することはできるが，文頭に置くのは不可。

(2) **1** より少ない活動 [名詞]   **2** より活動的でなく [副詞]
   ③ より活動的でなく [形容詞]   **4** 活性化がない [名詞]

   解説▶「become C（Cになる）」のCには，2つの品詞が置ける。「教師になる」のように，実際になるものを表す場合は名詞を，「活動的になる」のように，状態を表す場合は形容詞を置く。ここでは「私たちは鬱になり，（ 2 ）なるかもしれない」という状態を表しているため，形容詞の **3** が正解となる。

(3) **1** 選び出すかもしれない   **2** 来るべき
   ③ いまだにつきまとうかもしれない   **4** することができる

   解説▶直前の第1段落第10文「嫌悪感は，それ（嫌悪感）を引き起こしたできごとの記憶よりもはるかに長く続く長期的な潜在記憶となるかもしれない」より，「子供の頃高い壁から落ちて足首をひどく捻挫したときのことはもはや覚えていないかもしれないが，高いところへの恐怖は（ 3 ）のだ」は，痛みに関する記憶はなくしても，脳は覚えているという内容になると判断できる。よって，**3** が正解となる。

78

(4)　1　だけでなく　　　　　2　いくつかの点で
　　　3　さもないと　　　　　④　しかし

解説▶「脳には積極的に痛みの知覚をときには数分間，ときには数日間にわたり抑制する領域がある。（ 4 ），逆のことをし，私たちを痛みに対して過敏にさせる領域もまた存在する」より，**脳には痛みを抑制する領域と痛みに対して過敏にさせる領域という相反する領域があることが読み取れる**。よって，**逆の内容を接続する 4** が正解となる。

(5)　1　大破　　　　　　　　②　不快感
　　　3　消去　　　　　　　　4　無力

解説▶第3段落は，**過去と現在の対比関係に注目する**。**過去：乳児は痛みを感じないのではないかと思われていた，現在：乳児は痛みを感じる**ことがわかっていることから，「今日（子供がいる人なら誰でも肯定するだろうが），痛みを感じている乳児は明らかな（ 5 ）を示すだろうことはよく理解されている」は，**乳児は痛みを感じている**という内容になるため，**2** が正解となる。

正　解

No.	(1)	(2)	(3)	(4)	(5)
配点	10点	10点	10点	10点	10点
解答欄	3	3	3	4	2

| 得点 | (1回目) /50点 | (2回目) | (3回目) | CHECK YOUR LEVEL | 0〜30点 ➡ *Work harder!*
31〜40点 ➡ *OK!*
41〜50点 ➡ *Way to go!* |

Lesson 07
構造分析

[ ]=名詞　　□=修飾される名詞　<　>=形容詞・同格　(　)=副詞
S=主語　V=動詞　O=目的語　C=補語　'=従節

❶ [The perception] <of pain> is so fundamental (to our survival) (that it affects our brains (in profound ways)). There is (not) one single pain center; (instead), the whole brain lights (up) (like a Christmas tree) (when pain is perceived). (In the short term) we are (immediately) prompted (to protect the painful area), (to remove it (from [the source] <of the pain>) and (often) (to cease [all use] <of the affected area>) (while we examine it). (In the longer term), our subconscious behavior is altered. (If we hit our head (on a specific low beam or handle)), (next time) we'll duck. [An experience] <of pain> <that lasts (for long, continuous periods)> may affect our emotions and attitudes. We may develop depression and become less active. (Alternatively), [a severe experience] <of pain> and [a conscious awareness] <of (exactly) [what led (to that pain)]> may result (in [the development] <of [an aversion] <to [anything] <resembling the cause>>>). We call that aversion fear. The aversion may become [a long-term subconscious memory] <that lasts (far longer) (than [your memory] <of [the event] <that caused it>>)>. You may (no longer) remember [the time] <you fell (off the high wall) and (painfully) twisted your ankle (as a child)>, but [your fear] <of heights> may (still) be (with you).

【和訳】

❶ 痛みを知覚することは我々の生存にとって非常に重要であるので,それは私たちの脳に深く影響する。痛みを感じる中枢は1つではなく,その代わりに,痛みを感じると脳全体がクリスマスツリーのように点灯する。短期的には,影響を受けた部位を調べている間,私たちは痛みを感じる部位を即座に保護し,その部位を痛みの元から取り除き,しばしば影響を受けた部位のすべての使用を止めるように促される。長期的には,私たちの潜在意識の行動が変えられる。もし頭をある低い梁や取っ手にぶつけると,次回私たちは屈むようになるだろう。長期間連続して持続する痛みの経験は,私たちの感情と態度に影響を与えるかもしれない。私たちは鬱になり,あまり活動的でなくなるかもしれない。あるいは痛みに関してのひどい経験と,まさにその痛みを引き起こしたものを意識的に自覚することにより,その(痛みの)原因と似ているものには何に対しても強い嫌悪感を抱く結果になるかもしれない。私たちはその嫌悪感を恐怖と呼ぶ。嫌悪感は,それ(嫌悪感)を引き起こしたできごとの記憶よりもはるかに長く続く長期的な潜在記憶となるかもしれない。子供の頃高い壁から落ちて足首をひどく捻挫したときのことはもはや覚えていないかもしれないが,高いところへの恐怖はいまだにつきまとうかもしれないのだ。

重要語句リスト

語句	品詞	意味
perception	名	知覚,認識
fundamental	形	重要な,基本的な
survival	名	生存
perceive	動	感じる
in the short term	熟	短期的に
immediately	副	即座に,すぐに
prompt ~ to V	熟	~にVするように促す
painful	形	痛みを感じる
source	名	元,原因,源
cease	動	止める
subconscious	形	潜在意識の
behavior	名	行動,ふるまい
alter	動	変える
beam	名	梁
handle	名	取っ手
duck	動	屈む
last	動	続く
emotion	名	感情
attitude	名	態度
depression	名	鬱,不況
alternatively	副	あるいは
severe	形	ひどい,厳しい
conscious	形	意識的な
awareness	名	自覚すること
exactly	副	まさに,ちょうど
result in ~	熟	結果として~になる
aversion	名	嫌悪感
resemble	動	似ている
fall off ~	熟	~から落ちる
twist	動	捻挫する,ねじる
ankle	名	足首
height	名	高さ,身長

❷ We do(n't) (always) perceive pain. (Even) (when the nerve cells are sending us pain signals), there are times <when it is more important (for us) (simply) [to run away], (rather than [roll (about) (on the ground) (in agony)])>. (So) there are regions <of the brain> <that (actively) inhibit our perception <of pain>, (sometimes) (for just a few minutes), (sometimes) (for several days)>. But there are (also) areas <of the brain> <that do the reverse, and make us hypersensitive (to pain)>. (When we're safe and recovering), such heightened sensations might, (for example), encourage us (to avoid [using the painful part] (while it heals)).

❸ (Astonishingly), there used to be considerable confusion (about [when we (first) start experiencing pain]). (A hundred years ago) it was (widely) accepted [that newborn babies (simply) did (not) perceive pain (at all)], (because their brains had (not) developed (sufficiently)). (Perhaps) (rather (cruelly) (by today's standards)), (for decades) many 'pin-prick' experiments were conducted (on sleeping infants) (in attempts <to understand the onset <of pain perception>>). Much confusion was caused (in those early experiments) (by the seeming lack <of sensitivity <of babies <straight after birth>>>), (which turned out to be (because the mothers had received anesthetics (while giving birth), and the babies received a small dose (via their umbilical cords)). (Today) (as anyone with children can affirm), it is (well) understood [that a baby <in pain> will show clear discomfort]. Crying, wriggling, fisting, large muscle movements, (accompanied (by clear respiratory and hormonal changes)) and erratic sleep, are (all) clear signs <of pain>. But those early scientifically flawed experiments (sadly) resulted (in a culture <that disregarded the pain <of babies> (for much too long)>, (despite the true scientific findings)).

❷ 私たちは常に痛みを知覚するとは限らない。神経細胞が痛みの信号を私たちに送っているときでさえ，ただ逃げることの方が，激しい痛みで地面を転げ回るよりも重要なときがある。そのため，脳には積極的に痛みの知覚をときには数分間，ときには数日間にわたり抑制する領域がある。しかし，逆のことをし，私たちを痛みに対して過敏にさせる領域もまた存在する。例えば，危機を脱し回復しつつあるときになると，その過敏になった感覚により我々は痛む部分が治っている間はその部分を使わないように促進するかもしれない。

❸ 驚くことに，かつては痛みを最初に体験し始めるのはいつかということに関してかなりの混乱があった。100年前は，新生児は脳が十分に発達していないので全く痛みを感じないという説が広く受け入れられていた。今の規範からすればかなり残酷かもしれないが，何十年にもわたり，（人が）痛みをいつ感じ始めるのかを理解しようとして，「針つつき」の実験が眠っている乳児に対して数多く行われた。そのような初期の実験においては，生まれた直後の乳児は一見，刺激を感じることがないように見えたので，多くの混乱が引き起こされたが，それは母親が出産時に麻酔を受けており，乳児もへその緒を通して少量の麻酔を受け取っていたからだと明らかになった。今日（子供がいる人なら誰でも肯定するだろうが），痛みを感じている乳児は明らかな不快感を示すだろうことはよく理解されている。泣くこと，のたうちまわること，拳を握ること，筋肉が大きく動くこと，それに伴う明らかな呼吸とホルモンの変化そして一定しない眠りは，すべて痛みを感じている明らかな合図である。しかし正当な科学的な研究結果にもかかわらず，そのような初期の科学的に間違った実験は，悲しいことにあまりにも長期にわたり乳児の痛みを無視する文化という結果になってしまった。

☐ nerve cell	名	神経細胞
☐ signal	名	信号
☐ it is important for ～ to V	熟	～にとってVすることが重要だ
☐ roll about	熟	転げ回る
☐ in agony	熟	激しい痛みで
☐ region	名	領域，地域
☐ actively	副	積極的に，活動的に
☐ inhibit	動	抑制する
☐ reverse	名	逆のこと
☐ hypersensitive to ～	熟	～に過敏な
☐ recover	動	回復する
☐ sensation	名	感覚
☐ encourage ～ to V	熟	～がVするように励ます
☐ heal	動	治る
☐ astonishingly	副	驚くことに
☐ used to V	熟	かつてはVであった，Vするのは常だった
☐ confusion	名	混乱，曖昧さ
☐ accept	動	受け入れる
☐ sufficiently	副	十分に
☐ cruelly	副	残酷に
☐ decade	名	10年間
☐ conduct	動	行う
☐ infant	名	乳児，幼児
☐ attempt	名	試み
☐ straight	副	すぐに
☐ turn out to be C	熟	Cだと明らかになる
☐ anesthetic	名	麻酔
☐ dose	名	（1回分の）服用量
☐ via	前	～を通して，～経由で
☐ umbilical cord	名	へその緒
☐ affirm	動	肯定する
☐ discomfort	名	不快感
☐ muscle	名	筋肉
☐ accompany	動	伴う
☐ respiratory	形	呼吸の
☐ hormonal	形	ホルモンの
☐ erratic	形	一定しない，不安定な
☐ scientifically	副	科学的に
☐ flawed	形	間違った，欠点のある
☐ disregard	動	無視する

END

Lesson 08
問題文

■ Read the passage and answer the following questions.

Anger is "an emotional state that varies in (1) from mild irritation to intense fury and rage," according to Dr. Charles Spielberger, a psychologist who specializes in the study of anger. Like other emotions, it is accompanied by physiological and biological changes; when you get angry, your heart rate and blood pressure go up, as do the levels of your energy hormones, adrenaline, and noradrenaline.

Anger can be caused by both external and internal events. You could be angry at a specific person (such as a coworker or supervisor) or event (a traffic jam, a canceled flight), or your anger could be caused by worrying or brooding about your personal problems. Memories of traumatic or enraging events can also trigger angry feelings.

The instinctive, natural way to express anger is to respond aggressively. Anger is a natural, (2) response to threats; it inspires powerful, often aggressive, feelings and behaviors, which allow us to fight and to defend ourselves when we are attacked. A certain amount of anger, therefore, is necessary to our survival.

On the other hand, we can't physically lash out at every person or object that irritates or annoys us; laws, social norms, and common sense place limits on how far our anger can take us.

People use a variety of both conscious and unconscious processes to deal with their angry feelings. The three main approaches are expressing, suppressing, and calming. Expressing your angry feelings in an assertive — not aggressive — manner is the healthiest way to express anger. To do this, you have to learn how to make clear what your needs are, and how to get them met, without hurting others. Being assertive doesn't mean being pushy or demanding; it means being (3) of yourself and others.

Anger can be suppressed, and then converted or redirected. This happens when you hold in your anger, stop thinking about it, and focus on something positive. The aim is to inhibit or suppress your anger and convert it into more constructive behavior. The danger in this type of response is that if it isn't allowed outward expression, your anger can turn inward — on yourself. Anger turned inward may cause hypertension, high blood pressure, or depression.

Unexpressed anger can create other problems. It can lead to pathological expressions of anger, such as passive-aggressive behavior (getting back at people indirectly, without telling them why, rather than confronting them head-on) or a personality that seems (4) cynical and hostile. People who are constantly putting others down, criticizing everything, and making cynical comments haven't learned how to constructively express their anger. Not surprisingly, they aren't likely to have many successful relationships.

Finally, you can calm down inside. This means not just controlling your outward behavior, but also controlling your internal responses, taking steps to lower your heart rate, calm yourself down, and let the feelings (5).

As Dr. Spielberger notes, "when none of these three techniques work, that's when someone — or something — is going to get hurt."

(Controlling anger before it controls you. http://www.apa.org/topics/anger/control.aspx より一部改変)

Lesson 08
設問

Choose the best word or phrase from among the four choices to fill each gap.

(1) 1 intensity 2 space
    3 ratio 4 saturation

(2) 1 lucrative 2 lethargic
    3 adaptive 4 gentle

(3) 1 respectful 2 tragic
    3 exhaustive 4 ambiguous

(4) 1 merrily 2 profitably
    3 hardly 4 perpetually

(5) 1 subside 2 restrict
    3 limit 4 block

解 答 用 紙					
No.	(1)	(2)	(3)	(4)	(5)
配点	10点	10点	10点	10点	10点
解答欄					

Lesson 08
解答・解説

(1) **① 激しさ**　　　　　　　**2 場所**
　　3 比　　　　　　　　　**4 飽和**

解説▶「怒りは『軽いいらだちから猛烈な激怒や憤激に至るまで（ 1 ）が様々な感情の状態』である，と Charles Spielberger 博士，彼は怒りに関する研究を専門とする心理学者であるが，彼は言った」が文意。つまり，**怒りには様々な程度がある**ことが読み取れるため **1** が正解とわかる。

(2) **1 利益の上がる**　　　　**2 眠い**
　　③ 適応性のある　　　　**4 寛大な**

解説▶「怒りは脅威に対しての自然で（ 2 ）反応である。それ（怒り）は力強く，しばしば攻撃的な感情や行動を引き起こし，それにより，私たちは攻撃されたときに闘ったり自分自身を守ったりすることができる」が文意。**1・2・4** は文の流れに合わないため，消去法で **3** が正解とわかる。

(3) **① 敬意を表する**　　　　**2 悲惨な**
　　3 徹底的な　　　　　　**4 不確かな**

解説▶「自己主張をすることは，でしゃばりになることや自分本意になることを意味するのではなく，自身と他者に対して（ 3 ）ことを意味する」が文意。つまり**自己主張は，でしゃばりになることや自分本意になることなどの他者に対して遠慮のない態度とは違う**ことがわかる。よって，**1** が正解とわかる。

(4) 1 楽しげに 2 有利に
　　 3 やっと   ④ 常に

> **解説** ▶「それは受動的攻撃性行動（正面から立ち向かうというよりはむしろ，理由も言わずに，間接的に仕返しをすること）のような，不健全な怒りの表現や，（ 4 ）冷笑的で敵意があるように見える性格につながる可能性がある」が文意。続く前文の説明「常に他人をやり込めていたり，あらゆるものを批判していたり，冷笑的な批評をしている人々は……を身につけていない」より，空所を含む文は**「常に」そのような状態にある人**の説明をしていることが読み取れる。よって，**4** が正解と判断できる。

(5) ① 鎮まる   2 制限する
　　 3 制限する   4 遮断する

> **解説** ▶「これは，単に外側へ向かう自身の行動を制御することを意味するだけでなく，自身の内部で起こる反応を制御することや，心拍数を下げたり，自分を落ち着かせたり，その感情が（ 5 ）措置を講じることを意味する」が文意。直前の第 8 段落第 1 文を見ると「最後に，内面で落ち着くことである」と述べられていることから，空所を含む文は**内面で落ち着くことについて説明している**文だとわかる。よって，**1** が正解と判断できる。

正　解

No.	(1)	(2)	(3)	(4)	(5)
配点	10点	10点	10点	10点	10点
解答欄	**1**	**3**	**1**	**4**	**1**

得点	(1回目) /50点	(2回目)	(3回目)	CHECK YOUR LEVEL	0〜30点 ➡ *Work harder!* 31〜40点 ➡ *OK!* 41〜50点 ➡ *Way to go!*

Lesson 08
構造分析

[　]＝名詞　　▢＝修飾される名詞　　＜　＞＝形容詞・同格　　（　）＝副詞
S＝主語　V＝動詞　O＝目的語　C＝補語　'＝従節

❶ Anger is "an emotional state <that varies (in intensity) (from mild irritation) (to intense fury and rage)>," (according to Dr. Charles Spielberger), <a psychologist <who specializes (in the study of anger)>>. (Like other emotions), it is accompanied (by physiological and biological changes); (when you get angry), your heart rate and blood pressure go (up), (as do the levels <of your energy hormones, adrenaline, and noradrenaline>).

❷ Anger can be caused (by both external and internal events). You could be angry (at a specific person (such as a coworker or supervisor) or event (a traffic jam, a canceled flight)), or your anger could be caused (by worrying or brooding (about your personal problems)). Memories <of traumatic or enraging events> can (also) trigger angry feelings.

❸ The instinctive, natural way <to express anger> is [to respond (aggressively)]. Anger is a natural, adaptive response <to threats>; it inspires powerful, (often) aggressive, feelings and behaviors, (which allow us (to fight and to defend ourselves) (when we are attacked)). A certain amount <of anger>, (therefore), is necessary (to our survival).

❹ (On the other hand), we ca(n't) (physically) lash (out) (at every person or object <that irritates or annoys us>); laws, social norms, and common sense place limits (on [(how far) our anger can take us]).

❺ People use a variety of both conscious and unconscious processes (to deal (with their angry feelings)). The three main approaches are expressing, suppressing, and calming. Expressing your angry feelings (in an assertive — not aggressive — manner) is the healthiest way <to express anger>. (To do this), you have to learn [how to make clear [what your needs are]], and [how

90

【和訳】

❶ 怒りは「軽いいらだちから猛烈な激怒や憤激に至るまで激しさが様々な感情の状態」である，と Charles Spielberger 博士，彼は怒りに関する研究を専門とする心理学者であるが，彼は言った。ほかの感情のように，それは生理学的，生物学的変化を伴う。すなわち怒ると，エネルギーホルモン，アドレナリン，ノルアドレナリンの数値が上昇するにつれて，心拍数や血圧も上昇する。

❷ 怒りは外的なできごとと内的なできごとの両方によって引き起こされうる。特定の人物（同僚や上司のような）や，できごと（交通渋滞や飛行機の欠航）に対して怒るかもしれないし，怒りは個人的な問題を心配したりくよくよ考えたりすることで引き起こされるかもしれない。深く傷ついた（トラウマとなった）もしくはひどく怒らせるようなできごとの記憶はまた怒りの感情を誘発しうるのだ。

❸ 本能的で，自然な怒りの表し方は，攻撃的に反応することである。怒りは脅威に対しての自然な適応反応である。それ（怒り）は力強く，しばしば攻撃的な感情や行動を引き起こし，それにより，私たちは攻撃されたときに闘ったり自分自身を守ったりすることができる。したがって，ある程度の怒りは，生存にとって不可欠である。

❹ だが一方で，私たちは自身を怒らせたり，いらいらさせたりするあらゆる人や物を物理的に攻撃することはできない。法律，社会規範，常識は，どの程度まで怒りが私たちを占めることができるのかについて制限を設けている。

❺ 人々は，自身の怒りの感情に対処するために，様々な意識的，無意識的措置をとっている。３つの主な方法は，表現すること，抑圧すること，落ち着くことである。攻撃的ではなく，しっかりした自己主張を込めた方法で怒りの感情を表現することは，最も健康によい，怒りの表現方法である。こうするためには，他者を傷つけることなく，自

重要語句リスト

vary in ~	熟 ~が様々である
intensity	名 激しさ，強烈さ
mild	形 軽い，少しの
irritation	名 いらだち，立腹
intense	形 猛烈な，激しい
fury	名 激怒
rage	名 憤激
specialize	動 専門に扱う，特化する
accompany	動 伴う
biological	形 生物学（上）の
get angry	熟 怒る
heart rate	名 心拍数
blood pressure	名 血圧
external	形 外的な，外部の
internal	形 内的な，内の
coworker	名 同僚，仕事仲間
supervisor	名 上司
traffic jam	名 交通渋滞
cancel	動 欠航にする，取り消す
brood about ~	熟 ~をくよくよ考える
traumatic	形 深く傷ついた，トラウマとなった
enrage	動 ひどく怒らせる
trigger	動 誘発する
instinctive	形 本能的な
respond	動 反応する
aggressively	副 攻撃的に
adaptive	形 適応性のある，順応できる
threat	名 脅威，脅し
inspire	動 引き起こす，奮い立たせる
behavior	名 行動，ふるまい
defend	動 守る，防御する，擁護する
survival	名 生存
on the other hand	熟 一方で
lash out	熟 攻撃する，痛烈に批判する
object	名 物，対象
irritate	動 怒らせる，いらいらさせる
annoy	動 いらいらさせる
law	名 法律
norm	名 規範
common sense	名 常識
limit	名 制限
how far	熟 どこまで，どれくらい
a variety of ~	熟 様々な~，色々な~
conscious	形 意識的な

to get them met], (without hurting others). [Being assertive] does(n't) mean [being pushy or demanding]; it means [being respectful (of yourself and others)].

❻ Anger can be suppressed, and (then) converted or redirected. This happens (when you hold (in your anger), stop thinking (about it), and focus (on something positive)). The aim is [to inhibit or suppress your anger and convert it (into more constructive behavior)]. The danger <in this type <of response>> is [that (if it isn't allowed outward expression), your anger can turn (inward) — on yourself]. Anger <turned inward> may cause hypertension, high blood pressure, or depression.

❼ Unexpressed anger can create other problems. It can lead (to pathological expressions <of anger>, (such as passive-aggressive behavior (getting back at people indirectly, without telling them why, rather than confronting them head-on)) or a personality <that seems (perpetually) cynical and hostile>). People <who are (constantly) putting others (down), criticizing everything, and making cynical comments> have(n't) learned [how to constructively express their anger]. (Not surprisingly), they are(n't) likely to have many successful relationships.

❽ (Finally), you can calm (down) (inside). This means (not just) [controlling your outward behavior], but (also) [controlling your internal responses], [taking steps (to lower your heart rate, calm yourself down, and let the feelings subside)].

❾ (As Dr. Spielberger notes), "(when none of these three techniques work), that's [when someone — or something — is going to get hurt.]"

92

身の要求が何を明確にする方法や，それら（要求）をどのように満たすかを学ばなければならない。自己主張をすることは，でしゃばりになることや自分本意になることを意味するのではなく，自身と他者に対して敬意を表することを意味する。

❻ 怒りは抑圧され，それから変えられ，異なる方向に向けられうるものだ。これは，怒りを抑え，それについて考えるのをやめ，何か前向きなものに集中したときに起こる。その目的は，怒りを抑制，抑圧し，それをもっと建設的な行動に変えることである。この種の反応における危険性は，外側へ向かう表現が許されないなら，その怒りは内側，つまりは自分自身に向かう可能性があることだ。内側へ向いた怒りは，極度の精神緊張，高血圧，また鬱を引き起こすかもしれない。

❼ 表に出されない怒りは，ほかの問題を生み出すかもしれない。それは受動的攻撃性行動（正面から立ち向かうというよりはむしろ，理由も言わずに，間接的に仕返しをすること）のような，不健全な怒りの表現や，常に冷笑的で敵意があるように見える性格につながる可能性がある。常に他人をやり込めていたり，あらゆるものを批判していたり，冷笑的な批評をしている人々は，自身の怒りを建設的に表現する方法を身につけていない。驚くべきことではないが，彼らはあまり成功した人間関係を築けない傾向にある。

❽ 最後に，内面で落ち着くことである。これは，単に外側へ向かう自身の行動を制御することを意味するだけでなく，自身の内部で起こる反応を制御することや，心拍数を下げたり，自分を落ち着かせたり，その感情が鎮まる措置を講じることを意味する。

❾ Spielberger 博士が言及しているように，「こうした3つの方法がどれもうまく機能しないとき，それは誰かが，もしくは何かが傷つけられようとしているときなのである。」

☐ unconscious	形	無意識の
☐ deal with ~	熟	~に対処する，~を扱う
☐ approach	名	方法，取り組み
☐ suppress	動	抑圧する，鎮圧する
☐ calm	動	落ち着く
☐ assertive	形	しっかり自己主張する
☐ pushy	形	でしゃばりの，厚かましい
☐ demanding	形	自分本意の
☐ respectful of ~	熟	~に敬意を表す
☐ convert	動	変える，転換する
☐ redirect	動	向け直す
☐ hold in ~	熟	(感情などを)抑える，表に出さない
☐ focus on ~	熟	~に集中する，~に焦点を合わせる
☐ aim	名	目的，狙い
☐ inhibit	動	抑制する
☐ constructive	形	建設的な
☐ outward	形	外側へ向かう，外へ
☐ inward	形	内側へ向かう，内へ
☐ hypertension	名	高血圧
☐ depression	名	鬱，不況
☐ pathological	形	不健全な，理不尽な
☐ passive-aggressive	形	受動攻撃性の
☐ get back at ~	熟	~に仕返しをする
☐ indirectly	副	間接的に
☐ A rather than B	熟	B よりはむしろ A
☐ confront	動	立ち向かう，直面する
☐ head-on	副	正面から
☐ perpetually	副	常に，永久に
☐ cynical	形	冷笑的な
☐ hostile	形	敵意のある
☐ constantly	副	常に，絶えず
☐ put ~ down	熟	~をやり込める
☐ criticize	動	批判する，非難する
☐ comment	名	批評
☐ constructively	副	建設的に
☐ calm ~ down	熟	~を落ち着かせる
☐ subside	動	鎮まる，おさまる
☐ note	動	言及する，気づく
☐ get hurt	熟	傷つく

Read the passage and answer the following questions.

Owning a pet helps make people happier and healthier, lowering blood pressure, and delaying ageing. But there are some benefits for communities, too, according to a psychologist Pauleen Bennett, and they go beyond just saving Australia's health system an estimated $2.2 billion a year.

"Pets help us to feel better about our lives, and when we feel better about our lives, we feel more willing to do great things for our community," she says. Imagine a future with more pets in our cities, schools, and workplaces — where Buster the dog might sit by you in the office, and Polly the parrot* is part of the classroom. Imagine high-rise buildings and homes for the elderly with no bans on pets. Imagine even rental housing where creatures of all sizes are permitted.

This vision of the future is no mere fancy for Professor Bennett. "My grand plan to save the planet is to have more pets." As the new president of the International Society for Anthrozoology*, a field of research into human-animal interactions, she is gaining support for her case.

"We have 33 million pets in Australia," Professor Bennett says, so about two-thirds of all households, mostly families, have at least one pet. That is one of the highest rates of pet ownership in the world, but Australia's pet population stopped growing about a decade ago, according to the Australian Companion Animal Council. Official data show the number of dogs fell almost 10 percent between 1994 and 2009, while the cat population dropped nearly 20 percent.

Not everyone wants a pet, but research shows most Australians do. Eight in ten have lived with a pet, and of those who don't, more than half wish they did. So what's going wrong? "Our changing lifestyles are making it more difficult to own pets," Professor Bennett says. "As our society becomes more urban, the opportunities for natural contact with animals are becoming limited. So we need to make it easier for city people to own pets or interact with animals in other ways."

　　　Although pets take time and effort, there are ways around the problem: sharing a pet between families, adopting an older dog that requires less exercise, or choosing an independent animal like a cat. "Miniature goats make wonderful pets for people with small yards; if you can, please get two so that they can have company. Furthermore, rabbits, hamsters, and even goldfish make great pets for people who can't spend a lot of time at home. As a community, there are many different strategies we can try to make pet ownership easier," she says.

　　　Last year she took up a position at La Trobe University, where she now has room to keep ten dogs and a cat. At this university, she has a student surveying more than 1000 people on their relationships with pet parrots, and another looking at how pets can aid the coping skills of people fighting cancer. "There are five things that make life better for people: positive emotion, involvement, relationships, meaning, and achievement. It turns out that pets are helpful in all these ways," she says.

* parrot（オウム）　　anthrozoology（ヒトと動物の関係学）

Lesson 09
設問

(1) In paragraph 1, why does the author mention the Australian healthcare system?

    1 To show how it could be improved through technologies

    2 To recommend a method that could reduce its costs

    3 To clarify a public misunderstanding about its budget

    4 To suggest that having a pet brings some merits for societies

(2) According to professor Bennett, what has reduced the pet population in Australia?

    1 Most Australians already own too many cats or dogs.

    2 People no longer much wish to own animals.

    3 Modern lifestyles are too busy to include pets.

    4 People are increasingly living in urban residences.

(3) All of the following are described as pet-owning strategies by Professor Bennett EXCEPT

1 families taking joint responsibility for an animal
2 governments aiding low-income pet owners
3 choosing pets that fit one's living space
4 owning animals that are more independent

(4) What would be the best title for the passage?

1 The benefits and risks of pet ownership
2 The ways to maintain animal health
3 How to find the right pet care services
4 The necessity of owning animal companions

No.	(1)	(2)	(3)	(4)
配点	10点	10点	10点	20点
解答欄				

解答用紙

Lesson 09
解答・解説

(1) 第1段落で,著者がオーストラリアの健康管理制度に言及しているのはなぜか。
1 科学技術を通して,それがいかに改善されうるかを示すため
2 その費用を減らしうる方法を奨励するため
3 その予算について,公衆の誤解を明らかにするため
④ ペットを飼うことが社会に対するいくつかの利点をもたらすことを示すため

解説▶第1段落第1文「ペットを飼うことは,血圧を下げ,老化を遅らせて,人々をより幸せで健康的にするのに役立つものだ……地域社会に対しても恩恵があり」とある。つまり,ペットを飼うことは,人々を健康的にし,オーストラリアの健康管理制度にかかる費用を削減するのだとわかる。よって,**ペットを飼うことによる健康面への恩恵の度合いを,オーストラリアの健康管理制度になぞらえて表している**と読み取れるため,**4** が正解とわかる。

(2) Bennett 教授によると,何がオーストラリアのペットの数を減らしているのか。
1 大多数のオーストラリア人はすでに多すぎるほどの猫か犬を飼っている。
2 人々はもはや動物を飼いたいとあまり思っていない。
③ 現代の生活様式は多忙すぎてペットを飼うことができない。
4 人々は都市部の住宅にますます住むようになってきている。

解説▶第5段落第4文「**生活様式の変化がペットを飼うのをより難しくしている**」より,**3** が正解とわかる。**4** は同段落5文に「社会がより都市化するにつれ」とあるが,同段落6文「都市の人々がペットを飼ったり,動物と交流したりしやすくする必要があります」より,社会の都市化によって都市の人々が動物と自然に交流する機会が限られてしまうことが原因なのであり,社会の都市化は直接的原因ではないため不可。

(3) ……以外，以下のすべてはペットを飼う方策として Bennett 教授によって述べられている。
　1　複数の家族間で動物に対する連帯責任を負うこと
　②　政府が低所得のペットの飼い主を支援すること
　3　自分の生活空間に適するペットを選ぶこと
　4　より自主性のある［手のかからない］動物を飼うこと

解説▶ 1 は第6段落コロン（：）直後「ペットを複数の家族の間で共有する」，3 は第6段落第2文「小ヤギは小さな庭のある人に大変適したペット」，4 は第6段落第1文後半「猫のような自主性のある動物を選ぶこと」で触れられている。よって，**2** が正解となる。

(4) 本文に最も適するタイトルは何か。
　1　ペット所有の恩恵とリスク
　2　動物の健康を維持する方法
　3　適切なペットケアサービスの見つけ方
　④　動物の仲間を飼うことの必要性

解説▶タイトルは全体的な内容を一言で表現したものを選ぶ。本文は，ペットを飼うことで人が得られる恩恵などに触れながら，人々に対して**ペットの必要性**を訴えている。よって，**4** が正解となる。

No.	正　解			
	(1)	(2)	(3)	(4)
配点	10点	10点	10点	20点
解答欄	**4**	**3**	**2**	**4**

| 得点 | (1回目) /50点 | (2回目) | (3回目) | CHECK YOUR LEVEL | 0〜30点 ➡ *Work harder!*
31〜40点 ➡ *OK!*
41〜50点 ➡ *Way to go!* |

Lesson 09
構造分析

[ ]＝名詞　□＝修飾される名詞　＜ ＞＝形容詞・同格　（ ）＝副詞
S＝主語　V＝動詞　O＝目的語　C＝補語　'＝従節

❶ [Owning a pet] helps make people happier and healthier, (lowering blood pressure), and (delaying ageing). But there are some benefits (for communities), (too), (according to a psychologist Pauleen Bennett), and they go (beyond) (just [saving Australia's health system an estimated $2.2 billion (a year)]).

❷ "Pets help us (to feel better (about our lives)), and (when we feel better (about our lives)), we feel more willing (to do great things (for our community))," she says. Imagine a future ＜with more pets (in our cities, schools, and workplaces)＞ — (where Buster the dog might sit (by you) (in the office), and Polly the parrot is part ＜of the classroom＞). Imagine high-rise buildings and homes for the elderly ＜with no bans ＜on pets＞＞. Imagine (even) rental housing ＜where creatures ＜of all sizes＞ are permitted.＞

❸ This vision ＜of the future＞ is no mere fancy (for Professor Bennett). "My grand plan ＜to save the planet＞ is [to have more pets]." (As the new president ＜of the International Society ＜for Anthrozoology＞＞, ＜a field ＜of research ＜into human-animal interactions＞＞＞, she is gaining support (for her case).

❹ "We have 33 million pets (in Australia)," {Professor Bennett says}, so about two-thirds ＜of all households＞, (mostly families), have (at least) one pet. That is one ＜of the highest rates ＜of pet ownership＞ (in the world)＞, but Australia's pet population stopped growing (about a decade ago), (according to the Australian Companion Animal Council). Official data show [the number ＜of dogs＞ fell (almost 10 percent) (between 1994 and 2009), (while the cat population dropped (nearly 20 percent))].

【和訳】

❶ ペットを飼うことは，血圧を下げ，老化を遅らせて，人々をより幸せで健康にするのに役立つものだ。しかし，心理学者 Pauleen Bennett によれば，地域社会に対しても恩恵があり，それ（その恩恵）はまさにオーストラリアの健康制度を年間推定 22 億ドル節約する以上になるとのことである。

❷ 「ペットは，私たちを自分の生活に対して良い気分にさせ，そして生活に対して良い気分になると，地域社会に対して良いことを喜んで行おうとする気持ちになるのです。」と Bennett 教授は述べている。私たちの市，学校，そして職場に，より多くのペットがいる未来を想像してみよう。オフィスでは Buster という犬があなたの側に座るかもしれないし，オウムの Polly はクラスの一員になる。ペットが禁止されていない高層ビルと老人ホームを想像してみよう。どんな大きさの生き物も許される賃貸住宅も想像してみよう。

❸ この将来像は Bennett 教授にとって単なる想像ではない。「地球を守るための私の壮大な計画は，より多くのペットを飼うことである。」人間と動物の交流についての研究分野である，国際人間動物関係学会の新しい会長として，彼女は自身の主張に対する支持を得ている。

❹ 「オーストラリアには 3,300 万という数のペットがいます。」と Bennett 教授は述べており，すなわち全世帯の約 3 分の 2，そのほとんどは家族であるが，（彼らは）少なくとも 1 匹はペットを飼っているのである。これは世界でも最高のペット所有率の 1 つだが，オーストラリアペット審議会によると約 10 年前からオーストラリアのペットの数は増えていない。公式的なデータは，犬の数は 1994 年から 2009 年の間でほぼ 10% 減少し，一方で猫の数はほぼ 20% 減少していることを示している。

重要語句リスト

own	動 飼う，所有する
blood pressure	名 血圧
delay	動 遅らせる，延期する
ageing	名 老化，加齢
benefit	名 恩恵，利益
community	名 地域社会
according to ~	熟 ~によれば
psychologist	名 心理学者
go beyond ~	熟 ~以上になる，~を越える
estimated	形 推定の，およそ
billion	名 10 億
help ~ to V	熟 ~が V するのを助ける
willing to V	熟 喜んで V しようとする
workplace	名 職場
parrot	名 オウム
high-rise	形 高層の
ban on ~	熟 ~の禁止
rental	形 賃貸の
creature	名 生き物
permit	動 許す
vision	名 心に描く像，視力
mere	形 単なる，ほんの
fancy	名 想像，好み
grand	形 壮大な
planet	名 地球，惑星
president	名 会長
interaction	名 交流，ふれあい
gain	動 得る
support	名 支持，支援
million	名 100 万
professor	名 教授
household	名 世帯，家庭
mostly	副 ほとんどは，大部分は
at least ~	熟 少なくとも~
population	名 人口
decade	名 10 年間
the number of ~	熟 ~の数
between A and B	熟 A と B の間
drop	動 下がる，落とす
nearly	副 ほぼ，ほとんど

❺ Not everyone wants a pet, but research shows [most Australians do]. Eight <in ten> have lived (with a pet), and (of those <who do(n't)>), more than half wish [they did]. So what's going wrong? "Our changing lifestyles are making it more difficult [to own pets]," Professor Bennett says. "(As our society becomes more urban), the opportunities <for natural contact <with animals>> are becoming limited. So we need to make it easier (for city people) [to own pets or interact (with animals) (in other ways)]."

❻ (Although pets take time and effort), there are ways (around the problem): [sharing a pet (between families)], [adopting an older dog <that requires less exercise>], or [choosing an independent animal <like a cat>]. "Miniature goats make wonderful pets (for people <with small yards>); (if you can), please get two (so that they can have company). (Furthermore), rabbits, hamsters, and even goldfish make great pets (for people <who can't spend a lot of time (at home)>). (As a community), there are many different strategies <we can try to make pet ownership easier>," she says.

❼ (Last year) she took (up) a position (at La Trobe University), (where she (now) has room <to keep ten dogs and a cat>). (At this university), she has a student <surveying more than 1000 people (on their relationships <with pet parrots>)>, and another <looking (at [how pets can aid the coping skills <of people fighting cancer>])>. "There are five things <that make life better (for people)>: positive emotion, involvement, relationships, meaning, and achievement. It turns (out) [that pets are helpful (in all these ways)]," she says.

102

❺ 必ずしも全員がペットを欲しがっているわけではないが，大半のオーストラリア人は欲しがっていると調査は示している。10 人につき 8 人はペットと住んだことがあり，そうでない人でも半分以上がペットと住みたいと思っている。それでは，何がおかしいのだろうか。「生活様式の変化がペットを飼うのをより難しくしているのです。」と Bennett 教授は述べている。「社会がより都市化するにつれ，動物に自然と接する機会は限られてきます。したがって，私たちは，別の方法で，都市の人々がペットを飼ったり，動物と交流したりしやすくする必要があります。」

❻ ペットを飼うことは時間と努力を要するが，その問題に関する解決策はある。それは，ペットを複数の家族の間で共有すること，運動をあまり必要としない老犬を引き取ること，猫のような自主性のある動物を選ぶことである。「小ヤギは小さな庭のある人に大変適したペットです。できれば，仲間になれるように 2 匹で飼ってください。さらに，うさぎ，ハムスター，そして金魚でさえも，家で過ごす時間があまりとれない人にとっては良いペットです。地域社会として，ペットを飼うことを容易にするために試すことができる多くの様々な戦略があります。」と彼女は述べている。

❼ 昨年，彼女はラ・トローブ大学で仕事に就き，そこに（大学に）彼女は現在，犬を 10 匹と猫を 1 匹飼う場所を持っている。この大学で，彼女は，ペットのオウムと自身の関係について 1,000 名以上に調査をしている学生と，どのようにペットが，がんと戦っている人々の対処技能を助けることができるのかを調べている学生をもっている。「人々にとって，生活をより良いものにしてくれる 5 つのことがある。（それは）前向きな感情，関わり合い，結び付き，意義，そして達成です。ペットはこれらすべてにおいて役立つとわかっています。」と彼女は述べている。

go wrong	働 おかしい，うまくいかない
lifestyle	名 生活様式
urban	形 都市部の，都会の
opportunity	名 機会，好機
contact	名 接すること，接触
limited	形 限られた
interact	動 交流する，相互に影響する
take time	熟 時間を要する，手間どる
adopt	動 引き取る，採用する
require	動 必要とする，要求する
independent	形 自主性のある，自立した
miniature	形 小型の
goat	名 ヤギ
company	名 仲間
goldfish	名 金魚
spend	動 過ごす
strategy	名 戦略
take up a position	熟 職に就く，位置に就く
survey	動 調査する
aid	動 援助する，促進する
cope	動 対処する，乗り切る
cancer	名 がん
positive	形 前向きな，積極的な
emotion	名 感情
involvement	名 関わり合い
relationship	名 結び付き，関係
achievement	名 達成，偉業
turn out that S V	熟 S が V するとわかる
helpful	形 役立つ

END

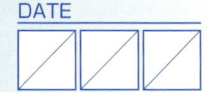

Read the passage and answer the following questions.

Have you ever wondered where fairy tales come from? Why are they so popular? Today, there are so many books about how fairy tales came to us. We now know that many of them began as simple stories. People shared them from one generation to the next but did not write them down. In those days, most people could not read or write. Storytelling was one of the most popular ways of passing time. These oral stories were called folk tales.

Each story had different versions, depending on who was telling it. For example, *Little Red Riding Hood* did not always have the same ending. Sometimes the wolf ate the little girl's grandmother. Sometimes a hunter killed the wolf and cut the grandmother, still alive, out of the wolf's stomach. These folk tales were not just for children. Many were scary and shocking. Often they tried to teach people about good and evil.

Later, people started to write down these stories and call them fairy tales. The Frenchman Charles Perrault, for example, is famous for his 1697 version of *Cinderella*. Usually, the stories came from older folk tales. Between 1700 and 1800 the demand for these stories and ones like them increased. One reason for this was that now, more and more people could read and write. Second, books were much cheaper. Third, people were more and more interested in their country's folk traditions.

Around 1800, the Brothers Grimm gathered old folk tales like *Snow White* and wrote them down. They changed the stories and made them more suitable for children.

Popular fairy tales, like *Snow White* and *Sleeping Beauty*, often had a message. Such messages reflected the cultural beliefs and values of that time. For example, both these stories showed a poor girl with a pure heart. In both stories she married a rich and powerful man to find happiness.

By 1900, fairy tales were part of children's lives. Teachers and parents welcomed new works of fantasy. Schools soon used *The Wonderful Wizard of Oz* (1900) and *Peter Pan* (1904) in classes. Walt Disney chose *Snow White* for his first animated color film. After its success, he continued turning fairy tales into films.

As times have changed, so have the messages in fairy tales. If we look at Disney's recent films, for example, we see a significant change. More and more of the leading characters are strong, independent women who actually have to rescue a man! In addition, there are many other new, exciting original stories like J.K. Rowling's successful *Harry Potter* series. Books like these show that our desire for both traditional and original works of fantasy is still growing.

Lesson 10
設問

(1) What does the author state about folk tales?

    1 They usually only lasted for one or two generations.

    2 They mainly continued in unwritten forms.

    3 They came from much earlier fairy tales.

    4 They began as factual historical stories.

(2) What is indicated about *Little Red Riding Hood*?

    1 It was considered evil by many traditional leaders.

    2 It was less shocking than similar fairy tales.

    3 It was shared among varied age groups.

    4 It was meant to have a consistent version.

(3) According to paragraph 3, which of the following statements about the period from 1700 to 1800 is NOT true?

    1 Demand for fairy tales increased among the populace.

    2 The number of people who could read and write rose.

    3 More people asked for social freedom from their leaders.

    4 Interest in national folk traditions became greater.

(4) It can be inferred from paragraph 4 that *Sleeping Beauty*

    1 challenged existing cultural beliefs.

    2 held a message about typical regional practices.

    3 encouraged readers to delay personal happiness.

    4 showed that wealth and power were not important.

(5) According to paragraph 5, what is true about *The Wonderful Wizard of Oz*?

   1 It became part of some academic courses.

   2 It displayed both fantastical and realistic parts.

   3 It emerged as the first animated color film.

   4 It sold much better than other fairy tales.

(6) With which of the following statements would the author most likely agree?

   1 The Brothers Grimm's fairy tale style was the best.

   2 Modern children dislike stories set in ancient days.

   3 Fairy tales remain an important part of modern culture.

   4 The demand for original stories is not being met.

解 答 用 紙

No.	(1)	(2)	(3)	(4)	(5)	(6)
配点	5点	5点	10点	10点	10点	10点
解答欄						

Lesson 10
解答・解説

(1) 筆者が民話について述べているのは何か。
1 民話はたいてい，1〜2世代しか伝承されなかった。
② 民話は主に，書き記さない形で伝承された。
3 民話は，はるかに初期のおとぎ話に由来していた。
4 民話は，歴史的実話として始まった。

解説▶ 第1段落最終文「こうした**口頭伝承**は，**民話**と呼ばれた」から，folk tales（民話）は**書き記さずに伝承**されていたことがわかる。よって，**2** が正解。

(2) 『赤ずきん』について述べられているのはどれか。
1 それは多くの従来の指導者によって邪悪だと考えられていた。
2 それは同類のおとぎ話ほど衝撃的ではなかった。
③ それはさまざまな年代で共有された。
4 それは終始一貫した作品解釈を持つことを意味していた。

解説▶ *Little Red Riding Hood*（赤ずきん）については，第2段落で述べられている。第5文「こうした**民話は子供たちのためだけのものではなかった**」より，**様々な年代へ向けたもの**だとわかる。よって，**3** が正解。

(3) 第3段落によると，1700年から1800年までの期間についての以下の陳述で正しくないものはどれか。
1 おとぎ話の需要が大衆間で増えた。
2 読み書きができる人の数が増えた。
③ より多くの人々が自分たちの指導者から社会的自由を求めた。
4 国の民族の伝統における興味がより増した。

解説▶ **1** は第4文「こうした物語のようなものの需要が高まった」，**2** は第5文「ますます多くの人々が読み書きできるようになった」，**4** は第7文「人々が自国の民族の伝統にますます関心を抱くようになった」にそれぞれ一致する。よって，**3** が正解とわかる。

(4) 『眠れる森の美女』は……と，第4段落から推察できる。
1 既存の文化的な考えに異議を唱えた

② 典型的な地域的な慣行についてのメッセージを含んでいた
③ 読者に個人の幸せを遅らせることを奨励した
④ 富と権力は重要ではないと示した
解説▶第 1 文で『眠れる森の美女』は教訓を備えていたことがわかる。続く第 2 文には「**そのような教訓は，文化的考えやその当時の価値観を反映していた**」とあるので，**2** が正解と判断できる。

(5) 第 5 段落によると，『オズの魔法使い』について正しいのはどれか。
① それは教育課程の一部になった。
② それは空想的な部分と現実的な部分の両方を示した。
③ それは最初のカラーアニメーション映画として登場した。
④ それはほかのおとぎ話よりもずっとよく売れた。
解説▶第 3 文「学校ではすぐに，『オズの魔法使い』(1900) や『ピーターパン』(1904) を授業で使った」より，**1** が正解と判断できる。

(6) 著者が最も同意しそうなのは以下の陳述のどれか。
① グリム兄弟のおとぎ話の形式が最高だった。
② 現代の子供たちは昔の設定の物語を嫌う。
③ おとぎ話は依然として現代文化の重要な一部である。
④ 独創的な物語に対する需要が満たされていない。
解説▶最終段落最終文「このような本は，伝統的で独創的なファンタジー作品に対する私たちの欲求がいまだに増加していることを示している」より，**4** が正解と判断できる。

No.	(1)	(2)	(3)	(4)	(5)	(6)
配点	5点	5点	10点	10点	10点	10点
解答欄	2	3	3	2	1	4

正 解

| 得点 | (1回目) /50点 | (2回目) | (3回目) | CHECK YOUR LEVEL | 0〜30点 ➡ Work harder!
31〜40点 ➡ OK!
41〜50点 ➡ Way to go! |

Lesson 10
構造分析

[　]＝名詞　　▢＝修飾される名詞　　＜　＞＝形容詞・同格　　(　)＝副詞
S＝主語　V＝動詞　O＝目的語　C＝補語　'＝従節

❶ Have you (ever) wondered [(where) fairy tales come from]? (Why) are they (so) popular? (Today), there are (so) many books ＜about [(how) fairy tales came (to us)]＞. We (now) know [that many ＜of them＞ began (as simple stories)]. People shared them (from one generation) (to the next) but did (not) write them (down). (In those days), most people could (not) read or write. Storytelling was one ＜of the most popular ways ＜of passing time＞＞. These oral stories were called folk tales.

❷ Each story had different versions, (depending (on [who was telling it])). (For example), Little Red Riding Hood did (not) (always) have the same ending. (Sometimes) the wolf ate the little girl's grandmother. (Sometimes) a hunter killed the wolf and cut the grandmother, (still alive), (out of the wolf's stomach). These folk tales were (not) (just) (for children). Many were scary and shocking. (Often) they tried to teach people (about good and evil).

❸ (Later), people started to write (down) these stories and call them fairy tales. The Frenchman Charles Perrault, (for example), is famous (for his 1697 version of *Cinderella*). (Usually), the stories came (from older folk tales). (Between 1700 and 1800) the demand ＜for these stories and ones like them＞ increased. One reason ＜for this＞ was [that (now), more and more people could read and write]. (Second), books were much cheaper. (Third), people were more and more interested (in their country's folk traditions). (Around 1800), the Brothers Grimm gathered old folk tales ＜like *Snow White*＞ and wrote them (down). They changed the stories and made them more suitable (for children).

【和訳】

❶ 今までおとぎ話がどこから来たのかを考えたことがあるだろうか。なぜおとぎ話はこんなにも人気なのだろうか。今日，おとぎ話がどのようにしてやってきたのかに関する非常に多くの本がある。今や，それらの多くは単純な話として始まったということが知られている。人々はある世代から次の世代へとそれらを共有したが，それらを書き記すことはしなかった。当時，ほとんどの人々は読み書きができなかったのだ。物語を話すことは，最も人気がある暇つぶしの方法の１つであった。こうした口頭伝承は，民話と呼ばれた。

❷ 各々の話は，誰がそれを語っているかによって，異なるものとなった。例えば，『赤ずきん』は必ずしも同じエンディングではなかった。ときには，オオカミは赤ずきんの祖母を食べた。ときには，猟師がオオカミを殺して，オオカミのお腹の中からまだ生きている祖母を救い出した。こうした民話は子供たちのためだけのものではなかった。（民話の）多くは恐ろしくて衝撃的なものであった。しばしばそれらは人々に善と悪について教えようとしていた。

❸ その後，人々はこうした話を書き記し始め，おとぎ話と呼ぶようになった。例えば，フランス人の Charles Perrault は，1697 年版の『シンデレラ』で有名である。たいてい，物語はより古い民話に由来していた。1700 年から 1800 年の間，こうした物語のようなものの需要が高まった。この理由の１つはすなわち，ますます多くの人々が読み書きできるようになったことである。第二に，本がずっと安価になったことである。第三に，人々が自国の民族の伝統にますます関心を抱くようになったことである。1800 年頃，グリム兄弟が『白雪姫』のような古い民話を集め，それらを書きとめた。彼らは物語を変え，それらをより子供向けにした。

重要語句リスト

wonder	動 ……かしらと思う，不思議に思う
fairy tale	名 おとぎ話
come from ~	熟 ~から来る，~に由来する
popular	形 人気がある
simple	形 単純な
share	動 共有する，分け合う
from A to B	熟 AからBへ
generation	名 世代
write ~ down	熟 ~を書きとめる
in those days	熟 当時
storytelling	名 物語を話すこと
one of ~	熟 ~の１つ
pass	動 過ごす，（時間が）経つ
oral	形 口頭の
folk tale	名 民話
each	形 各々の
version	名 版，説明
depend on ~	熟 ~による，~次第である
ending	名 エンディング，終わり
wolf	名 オオカミ
hunter	名 猟師
cut O C	熟 OをCにする
still	副 まだ
alive	形 生きている
stomach	名 腹，胃
scary	形 恐ろしい，怖い
shocking	形 衝撃的な
try to V	熟 Vしようと試みる
good and evil	善と悪
be famous for ~	熟 ~で有名である
usually	副 たいてい，通常
demand for ~	熟 ~への需要
increase	動 増加する
more and more S V	熟 ますます多くのSがVする
cheap	形 安価な，安い
be interested in ~	熟 ~に興味がある
tradition	名 伝統，慣例
around ~	前 ~頃
gather	動 集める
change	動 変える
make O C	熟 OをCにする
suitable	形 適した
such	形 そのような

Lesson 10

111

④ Popular fairy tales, (like *Snow White* and *Sleeping Beauty*), (often) had a message. Such messages reflected the cultural beliefs and values <of that time>. (For example), both these stories showed a poor girl <with a pure heart>. (In both stories) she married a rich and powerful man (to find happiness).

⑤ (By 1900), fairy tales were part <of children's lives>. Teachers and parents welcomed new works <of fantasy>. Schools (soon) used *The Wonderful Wizard of Oz* (1900) and *Peter Pan* (1904) (in classes). Walt Disney chose *Snow White* (for his first animated color film). (After its success), he continued turning fairy tales (into films).

⑥ (As times have changed), (so) have the messages <in fairy tales>. (If we look (at Disney's recent films)), (for example), we see a significant change. More and more <of the leading characters> are strong, independent women <who (actually) have to rescue a man>! (In addition), there are many other new, exciting original stories <like J.K. Rowling's successful *Harry Potter* series>. Books <like these> show [that our desire <for both traditional and original works <of fantasy>> is (still) growing].

❹ 『白雪姫』や『眠れる森の美女』のような人気のあるおとぎ話は、しばしば教訓を備えていた。そのような教訓は、文化的考えやその当時の価値観を反映していた。例えば、この話の両方には、純粋な心を持つ貧しい少女が登場した。また、両方の話において、その少女はお金持ちで権力のある男性と結婚し、幸せを見つけた。

❺ 1900年までに、おとぎ話は子供たちの生活の一部になった。先生や両親は新しいファンタジー作品を喜んで迎えた。学校ではすぐに、『オズの魔法使い』(1900)や『ピーターパン』(1904)を授業で使った。ウォルト・ディズニーは最初のカラーアニメーション映画に『白雪姫』を選んだ。その成功のあと、彼はおとぎ話を映画にし続けた。

❻ 時代が変わるにつれ、おとぎ話の中のメッセージも変わってきた。例えば、ディズニーの最近の映画を見れば、重大な変化に気づく。ますます多くの主要なキャラクターは実際に物語の中で男性を助けなければならない強くて自立した女性になっている。加えて、J.K. Rowlingの成功を収めた『ハリー・ポッター』シリーズ作品のような、新しく、わくわくさせる独創的な物語がほかにも多く存在する。このような本は、伝統的で独創的なファンタジー作品に対する私たちの欲求がいまだに増加していることを示している。

☐ reflect	⑩ 反映する、反射する
☐ cultural	⑱ 文化的な
☐ belief	⑫ 考え、信念
☐ value	⑫ 価値
☐ both	⑱ 両方の
☐ show	⑩ 現れる、示す
☐ poor	⑱ 貧しい
☐ pure	⑱ 純粋な、純正の
☐ marry	⑩ 結婚する
☐ rich	⑱ お金持ちの
☐ powerful	⑱ 権力のある、影響力のある
☐ happiness	⑫ 幸せ
☐ part of ~	⑲ ~の一部
☐ welcome	⑩ 喜んで迎える
☐ work	⑫ 作品、研究
☐ fantasy	⑫ ファンタジー
☐ soon	⑳ すぐに
☐ choose	⑩ 選ぶ
☐ animated film	⑫ アニメーション映画
☐ success	⑫ 成功
☐ continue to V	⑲ Vし続ける
☐ turn A into B	⑲ AをBにする
☐ as S V	⑲ SがVするにつれて
☐ so V S	⑲ SもまたVする
☐ recent	⑱ 最近の
☐ significant	⑱ 重大な、重要な
☐ leading	⑱ 主要な
☐ character	⑫ キャラクター、特徴
☐ strong	⑱ 強い
☐ independent	⑱ 自立した、自主的な
☐ actually	⑳ 実際、実は
☐ have to V	⑲ Vしなければならない
☐ rescue	⑩ 助ける
☐ in addition	⑲ 加えて、さらに
☐ exciting	⑱ わくわくさせる
☐ original	⑱ 独創的な、最初の
☐ successful	⑱ 成功した
☐ series	⑫ シリーズ作品
☐ desire	⑫ 欲求、願望
☐ traditional	⑱ 伝統的な

END

Special Column（生徒から東進講師陣に質問！）

Please teach me, teacher!

Q 英語の「4技能試験」では，何をどのように評価されるんですか？

A 4技能とは，従来の入試で出題されてきたReading・Listeningの2技能に，Writing・Speakingの2技能を加えた4つの技能のことです。それぞれの評価ポイントですが，Readingで求められている力は，本文の内容を読み込んでいくための語彙力と，英文の内容を頭の中でしっかりと構築する力です。細かい文法力ではなく，語彙力と英文の流れをきちんと追える力が重く評価されます。Readingには長文を読みその内容を答える問題だけでなく，長文の穴埋め問題や，語彙力を問う小問題が含まれることもあります。内容も学術論文のようなアカデミックな内容のものが多いです。

Listeningも，内容はアカデミックなシーンで使われるものが主流になりつつあります。例えば，学生と教授の会話や，講義のワンシーンを聴き取るというものです。リスニングでは，細かいところまで完璧に聴き取るということよりも，おおまかな流れをとらえ，会話の全体像を理解することが大切です。

Writingは，英文の要約や自身の意見を述べる形式が多いです。適切な語彙と文法を用いて英文を書くということが大前提で，そのうえで論理展開に一貫性があることが大切です。また，自分の意見を述べる場合は，その意見の根拠となる明確な理由をしっかり述べ，論理的な英文に仕上げることが高得点につながります。

Speakingにおいても，できる限り適切な語彙や文法を用いることが理想です。しかし，より大切なことは，語彙の選択や文法面で多少ミスがあったとしても，試験官ときちんと意思疎通をはかり，自身の主張を伝えきることです。また意見を述べる際は，Writing同様，その意見の根拠となる明確な理由を述べることが高得点の条件です。

最後に，4技能試験では，Reading・Listening・Writing・Speakingをバランス良く勉強することが高得点につながりますので，ReadingやListeningの勉強をしているときも，WritingやSpeakingに使えそうな表現を見つけたらメモしておくなど，すべての技能を統合させながら効率的に学習することをおすすめします。

（回答：東進英語科講師）

Premium Reading Workbook

Standard
STAGE-3
Lesson 11–15

Imperial College embodies and delivers world class scholarship, education and research in science, engineering, medicine and business, with particular regard to their application in industry, commerce and healthcare. We foster multidisciplinary working internally and collaborate widely externally.

Imperial College London

Lesson 11
問題文

■ Read the passage and answer the following questions.

The Swiss scientist Jean Piaget was the first to provide a detailed description of how a child's mind develops. He said that children's minds go through four main stages of development.

The first stage is called the "sensorimotor" stage and lasts from age 0 to age 2. "Sensorimotor" means the baby is in a world of senses (seeing, hearing, etc.) and movements. Babies first develop important movements, like drinking their mothers' milk. This act involves both the sense of taste and some movement. Later, babies use their sense and movements to learn about objects. For example, a baby recognizes that the chair it saw and touched the day before is the same chair it is seeing and touching today.

From age 2 to 7, the child is in the stage known as the "preoperational" stage. The word "preoperational" can be understood to mean something like "before one is able to think in the right way." Piaget called it "pre"-operational because he felt that the child was beginning to understand many things but still made many mistakes. Children in this stage can use language and can solve some problems, but they all make the same kinds of mistakes. For example, if you pour water from a tall, skinny glass to a short, fat glass, adults know that the amount of water is the same. But a child in this stage thinks that there is more water in the first glass because it is taller.

The third stage, called the "concrete operational" stage, starts at age 7 and continues through until age 11. In this stage, children begin to understand things like the glass of water test. Also, they become better at math, and can put groups of objects into sensible orders. They can also think about things from other people's points of view.

The last stage, from age 11 and up, is the "formal operational" stage. This is when children learn to think about things in more complicated ways. In this stage, children can learn advanced math or reasoning. They also learn to think about things like love and people's values in life. According to Piaget, some people never fully reach the formal operational stage. These people stay in the concrete operational stage for their whole lives.

Piaget's stages of childhood development, first described around 80 years ago, have been discussed a lot and changed. However, they still remain very useful for scientists today.

Lesson 11
設問

(1) Which of the following best describes the organization of the passage?

　1 A concept that challenges old beliefs

　2 A theory and its real-life details

　3 One idea and its main problems

　4 Comparing with explanations for an event

(2) According to the passage, all of the following are examples of the preoperational stage EXCEPT

　1 Making basic comprehension errors

　2 Getting lost within one's own home

　3 Correctly solving certain problems

　4 Using language structures

(3) What is indicated about the "glass of water test"?

　1 It is a measure of human reasoning ability.

　2 It is a problem that even some adults fail.

　3 It is easier for shorter people to do.

　4 It is based on mathematical principles.

(4) In mentioning "They also learn to think about things like love" is the author making which of the following points?

  1 All people naturally learn to love their parents.
  2 Some emotions require higher development.
  3 Individuals understand emotions differently.
  4 Complex emotions require advanced study.

(5) What would the author most likely claim about Jean Piaget?

  1 He acted as an outstanding educator of children.
  2 He rejected ideas that should have been considered.
  3 He developed a method for improving human brains.
  4 He designed a model that remains valuable.

No.	(1)	(2)	(3)	(4)	(5)
配点	10点	10点	10点	10点	10点
解答欄					

解 答 用 紙

Lesson 11
解答・解説

(1) 本文の構成を最もよく述べているのは以下のどれか。
1 古い考えに異議を唱えるある概念
② ある理論とその現実の詳細
3 １つの考えとその主要な問題
4 あるできごとの真相に似ていること

解説▶ 本文は，第１段落で「子供たちの心は４つの主要な発達段階を経験する」という**理論を述べ**，第２～５段落では，具体例を用いながら発達の第１～４段階について，その段階において子供ができるようになることの**具体例を挙げながら詳細を述べ**，第６段落で締めるという構成になっている。よって，**2** が正解となる。

(2) 本文によると，……以外のすべてが前操作期の例である。
1 基本的な思い違いをすること
② 自分の家の中で迷うこと
3 正確にある問題を解決すること
4 言語構造を使うこと

解説▶ the preoperational stage（前操作期）については第３段落に書かれている。**1** は第３文「子供が多くの物事を理解し始めるが，まだ多くの**間違いをすると感じた**」，**3・4** は第４文「この段階にいる子供たちは，**言語を使うことができ，いくつかの問題を解決することができる**」のように，例として挙げられている。よって，**2** が正解とわかる。

(3) 「グラスの水に関するテスト」について述べられていることは何か。
① それは人間の推論能力をはかるものである。
2 それは大人でさえも間違う人もいる問題である。
3 それはより背の低い人たちの方が容易にできる。
4 それは数学的原理にもとづいている。

解説▶ glass of water test（グラスの水に関するテスト）については第３～４段落に書かれている。グラスの水に関するテストを通してわかることは，**第３段落（発達の第二段階）では物事を理屈で考えることができないが，第４段落（発達の第三段階）ではできるようになる**ことが読み取れる。よ

って，**1** が正解。**4** は第4段落第3文「また，彼らは数学的な処理がよくできるようになり」とあるが，also（また）は「別の情報を追加する」働きをするため，glass of water test とは関連がない。

(4)　「彼らはまた，愛のような物事について考えることができるようになる」と述べる中で，筆者は以下のどれを主張しているか。
　1　すべての人が自分たちの両親を自然と愛するようになる。
　(2)　感情の中にはより高度な発達を必要とするものがある。
　3　個々がそれぞれに感情を理解する。
　4　複雑な感情は高度な学習を必要とする。
　解説▶該当する表現は第5段落に見られる。「愛のような物事」つまり「愛のような感情」は心の発達の最終段階である形式的操作期において発達するとそこでは述べられているので，**2** が正解とわかる。

(5)　筆者が Jean Piaget に関して最も主張したかったであろうことは何か。
　1　彼は子供の優秀な教育者としての役割を果たした。
　2　彼は考慮されるべきであったはずの考えを却下した。
　3　彼は人間の脳を改善する方法を発展させた。
　(4)　彼はいまだに価値のあるひな形を作った。
　解説▶最終段落「**子供時代の発達についての Piaget の段階**は，80年ほど前に初めて説明されたが，多くの議論が交わされ，変化してきた。しかし，それらは**今日の科学者にとってまだ非常に役に立つものである**」から，**4** が正解とわかる。

No.	(1)	(2)	(3)	(4)	(5)
配点	10点	10点	10点	10点	10点
解答欄	**2**	**2**	**1**	**2**	**4**

正　解

得点	（1回目） /50点	（2回目）	（3回目）	CHECK YOUR LEVEL	0〜30点 ➡ *Work harder!* 31〜40点 ➡ *OK!* 41〜50点 ➡ *Way to go!*

Lesson 11

Lesson 11
構造分析

[　]＝名詞　　□＝修飾される名詞　　< >＝形容詞・同格　　( )＝副詞
S＝主語　V＝動詞　O＝目的語　C＝補語　'＝従節

❶ The Swiss scientist Jean Piaget was the first <to provide a detailed description <of [how a child's mind develops]>>. He said [that children's minds go (through four main stages <of development>)].

❷ The first stage is called the "sensorimotor" stage and lasts (from age 0) (to age 2). "Sensorimotor" means [the baby is (in a world <of senses (seeing, hearing, etc.) and movements>)]. Babies (first) develop important movements, (like drinking their mothers' milk). This act involves both the sense <of taste> and some movement. (Later), babies use their sense and movements (to learn (about objects)). (For example), a baby recognizes [that the chair <it saw and touched (the day before)> is the same chair <it is seeing and touching (today)>].

❸ (From age 2) (to 7), the child is (in the stage <known (as the "preoperational" stage)>). The word "preoperational" can be understood (to mean something <like "before one is able to think (in the right way)>)." Piaget called it "pre"-operational (because he felt [that the child was beginning to understand many things but (still) made many mistakes]). Children <in this stage> can use language and can solve some problems, but they <all> make the same kinds <of mistakes>. (For example), (if you pour water (from a tall, skinny glass) (to a short, fat glass)), adults know [that the amount <of water> is the same]. But a child <in this stage> thinks [that there is more water (in the first glass) (because it is taller)].

【和訳】

❶ スイスの科学者 Jean Piaget は，子供の心がどのように発達するのかに関して詳細な説明を提供した最初の人物であった。彼は，子供たちの心は4つの主要な発達段階を経験すると述べた。

❷ 最初の段階は「感覚運動」期と呼ばれ，0歳から7歳まで続く。「感覚運動性」とは，乳児が感覚（見る，聞くなど）と運動の世界にいることを意味している。乳児は最初，母乳を飲むことのような，重要な運動を発達させる。この行動は味覚と運動の両方を含んでいる。その後，乳児は物について学ぶために，自分の感覚や運動を用いる。例えば，乳児は，前日に見て触ったイスが今日見て触っているイスと同じだということを認識する。

❸ 2歳から7歳まで，子供は「前操作」期として知られる段階にいる。「前操作」という語は，「人間が正しい方法で考えることができる以前」のようなことを意味すると理解されうる。Piaget は，子供が多くの物事を理解し始めるが，まだ多くの間違いをすると感じたので，それを「前」操作と呼んだ。この段階にいる子供たちは，言語を使うことができ，いくつかの問題を解決することができるが，皆同じ種類の間違いをする。例えば，背の高い細身のグラスから背の低い太目のグラスに水を注ぐと，大人ならば水の量が同じだとわかる。しかし，この段階の子供は，（最初のグラスの方が）より背が高いので，最初のグラスに多くの水があると考えるのである。

重要語句リスト

□ the first to V	熟 V した最初の人物
□ provide	動 提供する，供給する
□ detailed	形 詳細な
□ description	名 説明
□ mind	名 心
□ develop	動 発達する，展開する
□ go through ~	熟 ~を経験する
□ main	形 主要な
□ be called C	熟 C と呼ばれる
□ last	動 続く
□ from A to B	熟 A から B まで
□ sense	名 感覚
□ movement	名 運動，動き
□ important	形 重要な
□ involve	動 含む
□ both A and B	熟 A も B も両方とも
□ the sense of taste	名 味覚
□ for example	熟 例えば
□ recognize	動 認識する
□ touch	動 触る
□ the day before	熟 前日
□ something like ~	熟 ~のようなこと［もの］
□ be able to V	熟 V できる
□ in the right way	熟 正しい方法で
□ call O C	熟 O を C と呼ぶ
□ begin to V	熟 V し始める
□ make a mistake	熟 間違いをする
□ the same kinds of ~	熟 同じ種類の~
□ pour	動 注ぐ
□ skinny	形 細身の
□ fat	形 太った
□ adult	名 大人
□ the amount of ~	熟 ~の量

❹ The third stage, <called the "concrete operational" stage>, starts (at age 7) and continues (through until age 11). (In this stage), children begin to understand things <like the glass <of water> test>. (Also), they become better (at math), and can put groups <of objects> (into sensible orders). They can (also) think (about things) (from other people's points <of view>).

❺ The last stage, (from age 11 and up), is the "formal operational" stage. This is [when children learn to think (about things) (in more complicated ways)]. (In this stage), children can learn advanced math or reasoning. They (also) learn to think (about things <like love and people's values <in life>>). (According to Piaget), some people (never) (fully) reach the formal operational stage. These people stay (in the concrete operational stage) (for their whole lives).

❻ Piaget's stages <of childhood development>, <first described (around 80 years ago)>, have been discussed (a lot) and changed. (However), they (still) remain very useful (for scientists today).

❹ 第3段階は,「具体的操作」期と呼ばれ,7歳から始まり,11歳まで続く。この段階では,子供たちはグラスの水に関するテストのような物事を理解し始める。また,彼らは数学的な処理がよくできるようになり,対象群を目的にかなった順序に並べることができる。さらに,ほかの人々の視点から物事を考えることができる。

❺ 最終段階,これは11歳以上になってからだが,これは「形式的操作」期である。このとき子供たちは物事をより複雑な方法で考えるようになる。この段階では,子供たちは高度な内容の数学や論法を学ぶことができる。また,愛や人々の人生における価値観のような物事について考えることができるようになる。Piagetによれば,十分に形式的操作期に達しない人もいる。こうした人々は一生涯,具体的操作期にとどまることになる。

❻ 子供時代の発達についてのPiagetの段階は,80年ほど前に初めて説明されたが,多くの議論が交わされ,変化してきた。しかし,それらは今日の科学者にとってまだ非常に役に立つものである。

□ concrete	形 具体的な
□ continue	動 続く
□ through	副 ずっと,通り抜けて
□ put O C	熟 OをCにする
□ sensible	形 目的にかなった,賢明な
□ order	名 順番
□ from … point of view	熟 …の視点から
□ formal	形 形式的な,公式の
□ this is when S V	熟 これはSがVするときである
□ complicated	形 複雑な
□ advanced	形 高度な,進歩した
□ reasoning	名 論法,推論
□ according to ~	熟 ~によれば
□ fully	副 十分に
□ reach	動 達する,届く
□ stay in ~	熟 ~にとどまる
□ whole	形 すべての,全体の
□ childhood	名 子供時代
□ describe	動 説明する,記述する,述べる
□ however	副 しかし
□ remain	動 ~のままでいる,残る
□ useful	形 役に立つ

END

Read the passage and answer the following questions.

Though letters have been replaced by new technologies, there is nothing as valuable as a good letter. For hundreds of years, or at least since pens and paper became common, people who wanted to get in touch with other people separated by distance had only one way to do it: they wrote letters. Letters were the only means of long-distance communication, at least until the invention of the telegraph in the nineteenth century. Beginning with the telegraph, modern communication technologies such as e-mail have slowly but all too surely made letter writing one choice among many, and now merely an old-fashioned habit.

The decline in letter writing represents a cultural shift so large that in the future, historians may divide time not between B.C. and A.D., but between the eras when people wrote letters and when they did not. Historians depend on the written record. The purchase and sale of land, records of birth and death, weather reports, government documents — to the historian, nothing written is unimportant because it all contributes to the picture we have of the past. In the last century or so, historians have started to pay more attention to the lives of average people, arguing that the letters those people left behind are valuable evidence of how life was once lived. We know what our ancestors ate, how they dressed, and what they thought about, all from their letters. Reflecting on this, we can see how poorly historians of the future will be served by our generation, which produces almost no letters at all.

　　Although one reason we miss letters may be because we miss the simple world where letters were common by necessity, surely there is more reason for our fondness than mere nostalgia. When we read a letter, we develop an image of the letter writer unavailable to us in any other way. While Abraham Lincoln's speeches leave us admiring the man, his letters make us like him because we hear a plainer voice and obtain a more intimate view of his personality. He becomes more human to us. Moreover, his letters prove that the more we write, the more able we are fully to express thought and emotion. It is perhaps this intimate exploration and discovery of the self that we miss, something that no other form of communication yet invented encourages or supports.

(Malcolm Jones, "The Good Word," The Daily Beast, 2009/1/17, http://www.thedailybeast.com/newsweek/2009/01/17/the-good-word.html, 改変有)

Lesson 12
設問

(1) What is the purpose of the first paragraph of this passage?
1 To provide historical backdrop for a trend
2 To introduce an emerging theory
3 To compare explanations for a phenomenon
4 To critique the current consensus on an issue

(2) It can be inferred from the passage that one important purpose of written records is to
1 ensure that future generations maintain past cultural patterns.
2 prevent disorder from occurring within current governments.
3 create an archive of personal and social records.
4 supply people with hope for much better lives.

(3) According to the passage, what is NOT a result of the shift in communication?
1 A decrease in the number of letters
2 A lack of data for researchers
3 A new division of timelines
4 A loss of individual liberties

(4)　In paragraph 3, the author mentions Abraham Lincoln in order to

　　1　show how effective letter-writing can make a person great.

　　2　illustrate the longevity of very impressive speeches.

　　3　highlight how reading about someone humanizes them.

　　4　suggest that Lincoln ought to have written much more.

(5)　What is the best title for the passage?

　　1　The thoughts of leaders

　　2　The eternal value of a declining media

　　3　The necessity of education

　　4　The best way to speak

No.	(1)	(2)	(3)	(4)	(5)
配点	10点	10点	10点	10点	10点
解答欄					

解 答 用 紙

Lesson 12
解答・解説

（1） 本文の第1段落の目的は何か。
① ある傾向に歴史的背景を与えるため
2 ある新興の理論を紹介するため
3 ある現象の説明を比較するため
4 ある問題についての現在の統一見解を批評するため

解説▶ 第1段落第1文「手紙は新しい科学技術にとって代わられてしまっている」で**通信手段の傾向**について触れたあと，続く第2文以降で**手紙を中心とした通信手段の歴史**が述べられている。よって，**1** が正解。

（2） 本文から，文書記録の1つの重要な成果は……ことと推測されうる。
1 将来の世代が過去の文化傾向を維持すると保証する
2 現代の政府間で混乱が起こるのを妨げる
③ 個人的・社会的な記録についての保存記録の宝庫を作り出す
4 人々にはるかに良い生活のための希望を与える

解説▶ 文書記録の重要な成果については，第2段落で述べられている。第3文「土地の売買（の記録），出生と死亡記録，天気予報，公文書など，歴史家にとっては，過去の様子を引き出す助けとなるので，書かれているもので重要でないものは何もない」より，**人々が残した手紙は，歴史家たちに，個人的なものから社会的なものまで，膨大な量の史料を提供している点で重要であることが読み取れる**。よって，**3** が正解。

（3） 本文によると，情報伝達における変化の結果ではないものは何か。
1 手紙の数の減少　　　**2** 研究者のためのデータの欠如
3 年表の新しい区分　　**④** 個々の自由の喪失

解説▶ **1** と **3** は第2段落第1文「手紙を書くことの減少は，非常に大きな文化的変化を表しているので，将来歴史家たちが紀元前また紀元後でではなく，人々が手紙を書いた時代と書かなかった時代で区別するかもしれない」より不適切。**2** は第2段落最終文「将来の歴史家たちが，私たちの世代，それは，ほぼ全く手紙を書かない世代だが，この世代から与えられるものがどれほど乏しいか気づくことができるのだ」より不適切。よって，**4** が正解と判断できる。

(4) 第3段落によると、筆者は……ために、Abraham Lincoln について言及している。
1 効果的に手紙を書くことはどのように人を偉大にさせることができるかを示す
2 とても印象的な演説の寿命を説明する
③ ある人物についての読み物がどれほどその人を人情味あふれるものにするかを強調する
4 Lincoln がもっと多くのものを書くべきだったと示す

解説▶ 第3段落第1文後半「私たちの（手紙に対する）愛着には単なる郷愁の念だけではないさらなる理由が確かにある」より、第3段落は手紙に対する愛着の理由が述べられていると想定できる。第2文以降では Abraham Lincoln について言及しながら、**手紙は書き手に対するイメージを膨らませ、相手に好意を抱くこと**、続いて**その理由**、そしてその結果を「彼は私たちにとって、より人間らしくなるのである」としている。よって、**3** が正解と判断できる。

(5) 本文の最も適切なタイトルは何か。
1 リーダーの考え
② ある衰えている情報伝達手段の不変の価値
3 教育の必要性
4 最も良い話し方

解説▶ タイトルは全体的な内容を一言で表現したものを選ぶ。文全体は、手紙が新しい科学技術にとって代わられてしまっている現状を認めつつも、ほかの**通信技術**にはない**魅力**が手紙にはあることを、その理由を挙げながら述べるという流れである。よって、**2** が正解と判断できる。

正 解

No.	(1)	(2)	(3)	(4)	(5)
配点	10点	10点	10点	10点	10点
解答欄	**1**	**3**	**4**	**3**	**2**

| 得点 | (1回目) /50点 | (2回目) | (3回目) | CHECK YOUR LEVEL | 0〜30点 ➡ Work harder!
31〜40点 ➡ OK!
41〜50点 ➡ Way to go! |

Lesson 12
構造分析

[ ]=名詞　☐=修飾される名詞　< >=形容詞・同格　( )=副詞
S=主語　V=動詞　O=目的語　C=補語　'=従節

❶ (Though letters have been replaced (by new technologies)), there is nothing <as valuable (as a good letter)>. (For hundreds <of years>), or (at least) (since pens and paper became common), people <who wanted to get (in touch) (with other people <separated (by distance)>)> had only one way <to do it>: they wrote letters. Letters were the only means <of long-distance communication>, (at least) (until the invention <of the telegraph> (in the nineteenth century)). (Beginning with the telegraph), modern communication technologies <such as e-mail> have (slowly) but (all too surely) made letter writing one choice <among many>, and (now) (merely) an old-fashioned habit.

❷ The decline <in letter writing> represents a cultural shift <so large (that (in the future), historians may divide time (not) (between B. C. and A. D.), but (between the eras <when people wrote letters> and <when they did not>))>. Historians depend (on the written record). The purchase and sale <of land>, records <of birth and death>, weather reports, government documents — (to the historian), nothing <written> is unimportant (because it (all) contributes (to the picture <we have (of the past)>)). (In the last century or so), historians have started to pay more attention (to the lives <of average people>), (arguing [that the letters <those people left behind> are valuable evidence <of [how life was (once) lived]>]). We know [what our ancestors ate], [how they dressed], and [what they thought about], (all from their letters). (Reflecting on this), we can see [(how poorly) historians <of the future> will be served (by our generation)], (which produces almost no letters (at all)).

【和訳】

❶ 手紙は新しい科学技術にとって代わられてしまっているが，優れた手紙ほど価値のあるものはほかにない。数百年間，または少なくともペンと紙が一般的になって以来，遠く離れてしまった人と連絡をとりたいと思う人々がそれをする（連絡をとる）ための方法はたった1つしかなかった。手紙を書くことである。手紙は，少なくとも19世紀に電信が発明されるまでは，長距離通信の唯一の手段であった。電信に始まり，e-mailのような現代の通信技術は，ゆっくりと，しかしあまりに確実に手紙を書くことを多くの選択肢の中の1つに，そして今や単なる時代遅れの習慣にした。

❷ 手紙を書くことの減少は，非常に大きな文化的変化を表しているので，将来歴史家たちが紀元前また紀元後ではなく，人々が手紙を書いた時代と書かなかった時代で区別するかもしれない。歴史家は文書記録をあてにしているのである。（それは）土地の売買（の記録），出生と死亡記録，天気予報，公文書など，歴史家にとっては，過去の様子を引き出す助けとなるので，書かれているもので重要でないものは何もない。前世紀あたりから，歴史家たちは普通の人々の生活により多くの注意を払うようになり始めてきており，そのような人々が残した手紙は，昔はどのように生活が営まれていたかについての貴重な証拠であると主張している。私たちは，祖先が何を食べ，どのような装いをし，何について考えていたのかをすべて手紙から知ることができる。このことを熟考すると，将来の歴史家たちが，私たちの世代，それは，ほぼ全く手紙を書かない世代だが，この世代から与えられるものがどれほど乏しいかに気づくことができるのだ。

重要語句リスト

though S V	徶 SがVだが,SがVだけれども
replace	動 ～にとって代わる，取り替える
valuable	形 価値のある
at least ～	熟 少なくとも～
common	形 一般の，ありふれた，共通の
get in touch with ～	熟 ～と連絡をとる
separate	動 離す，分ける
long-distance	形 長距離の
invention	名 発明
telegraph	名 電信，電報
modern	形 現代の
surely	副 確実に，確かに
choice	名 選択
merely	副 単に，ただ
old-fashioned	形 時代遅れの，古風な
habit	名 習慣
decline	名 減少，衰え
represent	動 表す，象徴する
shift	名 変化
historian	名 歴史家
divide	動 区別する，分ける
era	名 時代
depend on ～	熟 ～をあてにする，～に頼る
record	名 記録
purchase	名 購入
weather report	名 天気予報
government document	名 公文書
unimportant	形 重要でない
contribute	動 寄与する，貢献する
pay attention to ～	熟 ～に注意を払う
average	形 普通の，平均の
argue	動 主張する，論争する
leave ～ behind	熟 ～を残す，置き去りにする
evidence	名 証拠
ancestor	名 祖先
dress	動 装いをする，服を着る
reflect on ～	熟 ～を熟考する
poorly	副 乏しい，ひどく
serve	動 与える，役立つ
generation	名 世代
produce	動 生産する，作る
no ～ at all	熟 全く～がない，少しの～もない

❸ (Although one reason <we miss letters> may be (because we miss the simple world <where letters were common (by necessity)>)), (surely) there is more reason <for our fondness> (than mere nostalgia). (When we read a letter), we develop an image <of the letter writer> <unavailable (to us) (in any other way)>. (While Abraham Lincoln's speeches leave us admiring the man), his letters make us (like him) (because we hear a plainer voice and obtain a more intimate view <of his personality>). He becomes more human (to us). (Moreover), his letters prove [that the more we write, the more able we are (fully) (to express thought and emotion)]. It is (perhaps) this intimate exploration and discovery <of the self> that we miss, something <that no other form of communication <yet invented> encourages or supports>.

❸ 私たちが手紙がないのを寂しく思う1つの理由は、手紙が必然的に一般的だった簡素な世界を懐かしく思うからかもしれないが、私たちの（手紙に対する）愛着には単なる郷愁の念だけではないさらなる理由が確かにある。私たちは手紙を読むときに、それ以外の（手紙以外の）方法では私たちに連絡をとれない手紙の書き手のイメージを膨らませる。Abraham Lincolnの演説により私たちは彼に敬服するが、彼の手紙により、私たちは彼のことが好きになる。というのも（その手紙を通して）私たちは、（Lincolnの）より飾り気のない意見を聞くことができるし、彼の人格についてより親密な見方ができるからだ。彼は私たちにとって、より人間らしくなるのである。さらに、Lincolnの手紙は、手紙を書けば書くほど、より十分に自分の考えや感情を表現できるようになることを証明している。我々が懐かしく思っているのは、おそらく、この手紙を書く自己に対しての深い探求と発見であり、それは既に発明された意思疎通のどの形でも促したり支持できないものである。

☐	miss	ⓓ 寂しく思う、逃す
☐	necessity	ⓝ 必然（性）、必要（性）
☐	fondness	ⓝ 愛着、愛情
☐	mere	ⓕ 単なる、ほんの
☐	nostalgia	ⓝ 郷愁、追憶
☐	unavailable to ～	ⓔ ～に入手できない
☐	speech	ⓝ 演説、話し方
☐	leave ～ Ving	ⓔ ～を…のままにしておく
☐	admire	ⓓ 敬服する、感心する
☐	make O V	ⓔ OにVさせる
☐	plain	ⓕ 飾り気のない、明白な
☐	obtain	ⓓ 得る、手に入れる
☐	intimate	ⓕ 深い
☐	view	ⓝ 見方、観点、景色
☐	personality	ⓝ 人格、個性
☐	moreover	ⓐ さらに、その上
☐	prove	ⓓ 証明する
☐	fully	ⓐ 十分に
☐	express	ⓓ 表現する、表す
☐	emotion	ⓝ 感情
☐	perhaps	ⓐ おそらく
☐	exploration	ⓝ 探求
☐	discovery	ⓝ 発見
☐	encourage	ⓓ 促す、励ます
☐	support	ⓓ 支持する、支える

Read the passage and answer the following questions.

　The idea of fighting over language might seem strange, but it's all too common. Why do people sometimes feel so strongly about their language that they are willing to fight against speakers of another? Why does language sometimes generate tensions that last for generations? The answers to these questions lie in the close relationship between language and identity, particularly ethnic identity.

　In many areas of the world, people of different language backgrounds interact every day. For the most part things go smoothly enough, but sometimes tensions arise, and sometimes these tensions erupt into outright conflicts. This is especially likely when speakers of one language feel threatened or oppressed by speakers of another. When that's the case, language differences become powerful markers of social, cultural, and political difference. And wherever you find language conflict, you're sure to find struggles over other issues as well, such as territory, religion, and political power.

　The weapons used in these conflicts may be far more than harsh words. Language conflicts can escalate into riots, wars, even genocide. Conflicts over language played a major part in the separation of Bangladesh from Pakistan in 1971. What began as a Bengali language movement escalated into a nine-month war for independence in which more than three million people died.

Language conflicts don't always lead to violence. But they can create tensions that persist for years, affecting the lives of millions on a daily basis. Take the case of Canada — generally a peaceful place, but one that has had its share of language conflict. Canada as a whole is officially bilingual, but most French-speaking Canadians live in the province of Quebec.* Surrounded by English-speaking provinces, they often feel that their language and culture are under siege. They feel particularly threatened by the presence of English speakers within Quebec itself, where historically, English speakers have been a powerful minority.

(E.M. Rickerson and B. Hilton (eds.), The 5 Minute Linguist, Equinox Publishing, 2006, pp.83-85, 一部改変）

* Quebec（ケベック州。カナダ東部の州の一つ。）

Lesson 13
設問

(1) According to paragraph 1, language

  1 is a potential source of serious discord.

  2 often limits the growth of ethnic groups.

  3 serves as the basis for discovering new identities.

  4 aids diplomats in avoiding unwanted conflicts.

(2) What conclusion can be inferred from paragraph 2?

  1 Multiple factors may interact to cause tensions.

  2 Some disagreements cannot be fundamentally resolved.

  3 Weapons can be negotiated away through diplomacy.

  4 Political power energizes religious belief.

(3) According to the author, the separation of Bangladesh and Pakistan

  1 exemplifies the need for more social movements.

  2 illustrates the unique role of independence fighters.

  3 shows how a situation can expand out of control.

  4 outlines the negative results of harsh language.

(4) What does the passage indicate about Quebec?
   1 Its laws restrict other Canadians from residing there.
   2 Its territory is the only bilingual province.
   3 Its English speakers are growing faster than French speakers.
   4 Its major population groups can be identified by language.

(5) What is the best title for the passage?
   1 A technical comparison of language forms
   2 The failure of recent international peace efforts
   3 A major cause of social divisions
   4 The dangers to linguistic minorities

No.	(1)	(2)	(3)	(4)	(5)
配点	10点	10点	10点	10点	10点
解答欄					

Lesson 13
解答・解説

(1) 第1段落によると，言語は……。
① 深刻な仲たがいを発生させる原因の1つだ
2 民族の発展をしばしば制限する
3 新しいアイデンティティーを発見するための基盤として役立つ
4 望まれていない闘争を避けるときに外交官を援助する

解説▶第1段落は「言語に関して争いをするという考えは奇妙に見えるかもしれないが，それは，あまりにも一般的である」という導入で始まり，続く文章では，「**言語と争い**」に関連づけて展開されている。よって，**1**が正解となる。

(2) 第2段落から推測されうるのはどの結論か。
① 複数の要因が互いに影響し合い，緊張状態を引き起こすかもしれない。
2 意見の相違点の中には根本的に解決できない点もある。
3 武器は外交を通じた交渉によって放棄されうる。
4 政治権力が宗教的信仰を活気づける。

解説▶第2文に「(異なる言語的背景が原因で)時々**緊張状態が生じ**，このような**緊張状態は，時々完全な闘争へと発展する**」とあり，最終文では「**言語闘争が見られる所ならどこでも，領土，宗教，政治権力のようなほかの問題に関する争いもまた見られるのは確実だ**」と述べられている。よって，**1**が正解と判断できる。**2**は「意見の相違点」のみを扱った選択肢だが，本文は「領土，宗教，政治権力のようなほかの問題に関する争い」も扱っているため不可である。

(3) 筆者によると，バングラデシュとパキスタンの分離独立は……。
1 より社会的な運動の必要性を例証している
2 独立した戦士特有の役割を例証している
③ いかに状況が制御不能なほどに拡大しうるかを示している
4 不快な言語の芳しくない結果を概説している

解説▶バングラデシュとパキスタンの分離独立については第3段落に書かれている。第2文で「**言語闘争は暴動や戦争，さらには組織的大量虐殺にまで悪化することがある**」と述べ，第3文はその具体例としてバングラ

デシュとパキスタンの分離独立を挙げている。よって，**3** が正解と判断できる。

(4) この文章ではケベック州について何と述べているか。
 1 州の法律により，ほかのカナダ人がそこへ居住することが制限されている。
 2 州の領土は唯一の2言語使用の州である。
 3 州の英語話者は，フランス語話者よりも速く増えつつある。
 ④ 州の主要な人口集団は言語によって識別されうる。

解説 ▶ Quebec（ケベック州）については，最終段落に書かれている。最終段落第3〜最終文より，**使用する言語により，仲間の集団とそうでない集団を区別することが読み取れる**。よって，**4** が正解とわかる。また，**1・2・3** は無記述のため，消去法で **4** を選ぶこともできる。

(5) 本文の最適なタイトルは何か。
 1 言語形式の技術的比較
 2 最近の国際的な平和への努力の失敗
 ③ 社会的区分の主な原因
 4 言語の少数派にとっての脅威

解説 ▶ タイトルは全体的な内容を一言で表現したものを選ぶ。文全体は，言語の違いが，争いや，長年続く緊張状態を生み出すという流れである。つまり，**言語は世界を区分する原因の1つであることが読み取れる**ため，**3** が正解となる。

正 解

No.	(1)	(2)	(3)	(4)	(5)
配点	10点	10点	10点	10点	10点
解答欄	**1**	**1**	**3**	**4**	**3**

| 得点 | (1回目) /50点 | (2回目) | (3回目) | CHECK YOUR LEVEL | 0〜30点 ➡ Work harder!
31〜40点 ➡ OK!
41〜50点 ➡ Way to go! |

Lesson 13
構造分析

[ ]=名詞　□=修飾される名詞　< >=形容詞・同格　( )=副詞
S=主語　V=動詞　O=目的語　C=補語　'=従節

❶ The idea <of fighting (over language)> might seem strange, but it's (all) too common. (Why) do people (sometimes) feel (so strongly) (about their language) [that they are willing to fight (against speakers <of another>)]? (Why) does language (sometimes) generate tensions <that last (for generations)>? The answers <to these questions> lie (in the close relationship <between language and identity, (particularly) ethnic identity>).

❷ (In many areas <of the world>), people <of different language backgrounds> interact (every day). (For the most part) things go (smoothly enough), but (sometimes) tensions arise, and (sometimes) these tensions erupt (into outright conflicts). This is (especially) likely (when speakers <of one language> feel threatened or oppressed (by speakers <of another>)). (When that's the case), language differences become powerful markers <of social, cultural, and political difference>. And (wherever you find language conflict), you're sure to find struggles (over other issues) (as well), <such as territory, religion, and political power>.

【和訳】

❶ 言語に関して争いをするという考えは奇妙に見えるかもしれないが，それは，あまりにも一般的であるのだ。なぜ，人々はときにほかの言語を話す人たちと戦いを起こそうとするほど，自分たちの言語について強い思いを持つのだろうか。なぜ，言語はときに何世代にもわたる緊張状態を生み出すことがあるのだろうか。これらの疑問に対する答えは，言語とアイデンティティー，特に民族のアイデンティティーとの密接な関係性の中にあるのだ。

❷ 世界の多くの場所では，日々，異なる言語的背景を持つ人々が交流している。ほとんどの場合，物事は十分に滞りなく進むのだが，時々緊張状態が生じ，このような緊張状態は，時々完全な闘争へと発展する。こういった事態は，ある言語の話者がほかの言語の話者からの脅威や圧迫を感じるときに特に起こりやすいようだ。それが事実であるとき，言語の違いは社会的，文化的，そして政治的な違いの強力なしるしとなる。そして，言語闘争が見られる所ならどこでも，領土，宗教，政治権力のようなほかの問題に関する争いもまた見られるのは確実だ。

重要語句リスト

fight over ~	~のことで争う
all too ~	あまりにも~すぎる
common	ありふれた，一般の，共通の
strongly	強く
be willing to V	Vしたいと思う
fight against ~	~と戦う
speaker	話し手
generate	生み出す
tension	緊張状態
last	続く
generation	世代
lie in ~	~にある
relationship between A and B	AとBの関係
identity	アイデンティティー，自己同一性，個性
particularly	特に
ethnic	民族の，民族的な
background	背景
interact	交流する，相互に影響する
smoothly	滞りなく，円滑に
arise	生じる，起こる
erupt into ~	~へと発展する，~へと爆発する
outright	完全な
conflict	闘争，紛争
especially	特に
likely	ありそうな，起こりそうな
feel threatened	脅威を感じる
feel oppressed	圧迫されていると感じる
the case	事実
marker	しるし
political	政治的な
difference	違い
wherever S V	SがVする所ならどこでも
be sure to V	Vするのは確実である
struggle	争い
issue	問題
~ as well	~もまた
A such as B	BのようなA
territory	領土，縄張り
religion	宗教
power	権力

❸ The weapons used (in these conflicts) may be (far) more (than harsh words). Language conflicts can escalate (into riots, wars, even genocide). Conflicts over language played a major part (in the separation of Bangladesh) (from Pakistan) (in 1971)). [What began (as a Bengali language movement)] escalated (into a nine-month war for independence in which more than three million people died)).

❹ Language conflicts do(n't) (always) lead (to violence). But they can create tensions that persist (for years), (affecting the lives of millions) (on a daily basis)). Take the case of Canada — generally a peaceful place, but one that has had its share of language conflict. Canada (as a whole) is (officially) bilingual, but most French-speaking Canadians live (in the province of Quebec)). (Surrounded (by English-speaking provinces)), they (often) feel [that their language and culture are (under siege)]. They feel (particularly) threatened (by the presence of English speakers) (within Quebec itself)), (where (historically), English speakers have been a powerful minority).

144

❸ このような闘争で用いられる対抗手段は，不快な言葉だけではない。言語闘争は暴動や戦争，さらには組織的大量虐殺にまで悪化することがある。言語に関する闘争は，1971年にバングラデシュがパキスタンから分離独立したときに重大な役割を果たした。ベンガル語運動として始まったものが，300万人以上の死者を出した9ヵ月にわたる独立戦争にまで悪化したのだ。

❹ 言語闘争は必ずしも暴力に結び付くとは限らない。しかし，何年も存続する緊張状態を生み出し，日々，何百万人もの生活に影響を与えることがある。カナダの場合を取り上げてみよう。概して平和な場所だが，言語闘争を経験した場所でもある。カナダは全体としては公式には2言語使用（の国）であるが，フランス語を話すカナダ人の大半はケベック州に住んでいる。英語を話す州に囲まれ，彼らは自身の言語や文化が包囲されているとしばしば感じている。彼らはケベック州内で英語を話す人々の存在にとりわけ脅威を感じている。（というのも）そこ（ケベック州）では歴史的に，英語を話す人が影響力のある少数の集団であった（からだ）。

□ weapon	名 対抗手段，武器
□ far	副 さらに，はるかに
□ harsh	形 不快な，厳しい
□ escalate	動 悪化する，拡大する
□ riot	名 暴動
□ genocide	名 大量虐殺
□ major	形 重大な
□ separation	名 分離
□ million	名 百万
□ lead to ~	熟 ~につながる，~へと至る
□ violence	名 暴力
□ persist	動 存続する，続く
□ affect	動 影響を与える，影響する
□ on a daily basis	熟 毎日
□ generally	副 概して，一般に
□ have one's share of ~	熟 ~を経験する
□ as a whole	熟 全体として
□ officially	副 公式には
□ bilingual	形 2言語使用の，2カ国語を話す
□ province	名 州
□ surround	動 囲む
□ under siege	熟 包囲されている
□ powerful	形 影響力のある，権力のある
□ minority	名 少数（派）

Lesson 13

END

Read the passage and answer the following questions.

　A star is a big ball of fire in space that makes lots of light and other forms of energy. A star is mostly made up of gases and something like fire, only much hotter. There are thousands of explosions happening all over the star all the time. This is where the star's heat and light come from. These explosions are also where a star gets its color from.

　Our sun is a star. It is the closest star to our planet, and it sends its energy to the Earth as heat and light. The sun seems large to us, but it is only a medium sized star called a yellow dwarf (small star). Other stars can be different colors. Some stars have more energy than our sun and burn even hotter than our sun does. Stars that are hotter than our sun may look blue or white. Stars that are cooler than our sun may look orange or red.

　Stars come in many sizes. Our sun is about 1.4 million kilometers around, but people still call it a dwarf because many stars are much bigger. For example, there are many stars which are more than 100 times bigger than our sun. The largest stars are called red supergiants. These stars are so big that most of our small solar system could fit inside one. If our sun turned into a red supergiant, its mass would extend out to Jupiter's orbit.

　Stars, just like people, have a life, but a star's life is much longer than a human's. The sun is billions of years old and will live for many more billions of years. When our sun starts to die, it will grow into a red giant star. It will not become a supergiant because it is not heavy enough. When our sun dies, it will get so hot that the heat and light will burn the Earth. In fact, it will be too hot for anything to live on the Earth when our sun becomes a red giant. Then, our sun will slowly get darker and colder until it stops giving off any energy at all.

Lesson 14
設問

(1) What is true about stars, according to paragraph 1?

　1 Their energy is reduced through constant explosions.

　2 They get hotter as they pull in more gases.

　3 Fires within them are constantly changing color.

　4 Gases make up some of their matter.

(2) Why does the author state "The sun seems large to us" in paragraph 2?

　1 To suggest that it is larger than it seems

　2 To compare it to medium-sized planets

　3 To show our subjective impression of information on its actual size

　4 To indicate that people have long studied space

(3) Which of the following best describes the organization of paragraph 3?

　1 An idea supported by examples

　2 One topic supported by others

　3 A discussion of different theories

　4 Several unrelated concepts

(4) The author states that red supergiant stars

1　regularly expand by millions of kilometers around.

2　could one day drift into the orbit of Jupiter.

3　are big enough to hold much of our solar system.

4　may enclose the energy of much smaller stars.

(5) According to paragraph 4, all of the following will take place as the sun dies EXCEPT

1　growth into a red giant

2　collapse into scattered material

3　burning of the earth's surface

4　eventual cooling down

解 答 用 紙					
No.	(1)	(2)	(3)	(4)	(5)
配点	10点	10点	10点	10点	10点
解答欄					

Lesson 14
解答・解説

(1) 第1段落によると、恒星について正しいものは何か。
1 それらのエネルギーは繰り返し起こる爆発を通して減少する。
2 それらはより多くのガスを引き込みながら熱くなる。
3 それらの中の火は繰り返し色を変えている。
④ ガスはそれらの要素のいくらかを構成している。

解説▶第1段落第2文「恒星の大半はガスやそれ（ガス）よりもずっと高温な火のようなもので構成されている」より、**4**が正解とわかる。**1・2・3**は無記述。

(2) 第2段落で筆者が「The sun seems large to us」と述べているのはなぜか。
1 それが思ったより大きいことを示すため
2 それを中型の惑星と比べるため
③ 実際のサイズ情報に対する我々の主観的な印象を示すため
4 人々が長い間宇宙を研究してきたことを示すため

解説▶第2段落第3文「太陽は我々にとっては大きいように見えるが、黄色矮星（小さな恒星）と呼ばれる中位的な大きさの恒星にすぎない」より、太陽の大きさに関して前半では**主観的な印象**が述べられているのに対し、後半では**客観的な情報**が示されていることがわかる。よって、**3**が正解とわかる。

(3) 第3段落の構成を最もよく説明しているのは以下のうちどれか。
① 実例によって支持された考え
2 そのほかのトピックによって支持されたトピック
3 異なる理論の議論
4 いくつかの無関係な概念

解説▶第3段落第1文「恒星には多くの大きさがある」から、この段落は恒星の大きさについて述べた段落であることが想定できる。大きさをふまえながら、第2文では矮星が、第4文では赤色超巨星が紹介されており、第6文の具体例が挙げられていることがわかる。よって、**1**が正解と判断できる。

Lesson 14（3／5）　問題文→設問→解答・解説→構造分析

(4)　筆者は，赤色超巨星は……と述べている。
　　1　周囲数百万キロメートルまで定期的に拡大する
　　2　ある日木星の軌道の中を漂うかもしれない
　　③　私たちの太陽系の多くを入れるのに十分な大きさである
　　4　はるかに小さな恒星のエネルギーを囲むかもしれない

　解説▶ 赤色超巨星については第3段落で述べられている。第5文「これらの恒星は非常に大きいので，私たちの小さな太陽系の大半がその1つの恒星の中に収まることもありうるのである」より，**3**が正解と判断できる。

(5)　第4段落によると，……を除く以下のすべてが，太陽が消えるときに起こるだろう。
　　1　赤い巨星への成長
　　②　まばらな物質へと崩壊する
　　3　地球の表面を燃やすこと
　　4　最終的に冷たくなること

　解説▶ 1 は第4段落第3文「太陽が消え始めるとき，それは赤色巨星へと発達するだろう」，**3** は第5文「太陽が消えるとき，それはとても高温になるのでその熱と光は地球を燃やすだろう」，**4** は第7文「その後，太陽は全くエネルギーを放出しなくなるまで，ゆっくりとだんだん暗く冷たくなるのである」でそれぞれ述べられている。よって，**2**が正解とわかる。

	正　解				
No.	(1)	(2)	(3)	(4)	(5)
配点	10点	10点	10点	10点	10点
解答欄	4	3	1	3	2

| 得点 | （1回目）／50点 | （2回目） | （3回目） | CHECK YOUR LEVEL | 0～30点 ➡ Work harder!
31～40点 ➡ OK!
41～50点 ➡ Way to go! |

Lesson 14
構造分析

[　]＝名詞　　□＝修飾される名詞　　＜　＞＝形容詞・同格　　(　)＝副詞
S＝主語　V＝動詞　O＝目的語　C＝補語　'＝従節

❶ A star is [a big ball] <of fire> (in [space]) <that makes [lots] <of light and other forms of energy>>). A star is (mostly) made (up) (of gases and [something] <like fire>, <only much hotter>). There are [thousands of explosions] <happening (all over the star) (all the time)>. This is [where the star's heat and light come from]. These explosions are (also) [where a star gets its color from].

❷ Our sun is a star. It is the closest star (to our planet), and it sends its energy (to the Earth) (as heat and light). The sun seems large (to us), but it is (only) [a medium sized star] <called a yellow dwarf> (small star). Other stars can be different colors. Some stars have more energy (than our sun) and burn (even hotter) (than our sun does). [Stars] <that are hotter (than our sun)> may look blue or white. [Stars] <that are cooler (than our sun)> may look orange or red.

❸ Stars come (in many sizes). Our sun is about 1.4 million kilometers around, but people (still) call it a dwarf (because many stars are much bigger). (For example), there are [many stars] <which are more than 100 times bigger (than our sun)>. The largest stars are called red supergiants. These stars are so big (that [most] <of our small solar system> could fit (inside one)). (If our sun turned (into a red supergiant)), [its mass] would extend (out) (to Jupiter's orbit).

【和訳】

❶ 恒星は多くの光とそのほかのエネルギー形態を生み出す宇宙における大きな火の玉である。恒星の大半はガスやそれ（ガス）よりもずっと高温な火のようなもので構成されている。その恒星の至るところでは常に何千もの爆発が起こっている。これにより恒星の熱や光は生まれる。この爆発はまた，恒星の色が由来するものでもある。

❷ 我々の太陽は恒星である。それは我々の惑星に最も近い恒星で，それ（太陽）は熱や光としてそのエネルギーを地球へ送っている。太陽は我々にとっては大きいように見えるが，黄色矮星（小さな恒星）と呼ばれる中位な大きさの恒星にすぎない。ほかの恒星は異なる色を持ちうる。太陽よりもエネルギーを持っており，太陽よりも高い温度で燃えるものもある。太陽よりも高い温度の恒星は青色や，白色に見えるかもしれない。太陽よりも低い温度の恒星はオレンジ色もしくは，赤色に見えるかもしれない。

❸ 恒星には多くの大きさがある。太陽は周囲約140万キロメートルであるが，多くの恒星は，それ（太陽）よりずっと大きいので，依然として人々は太陽を矮星と呼ぶ。例えば太陽の100倍以上大きな恒星も多くある。最大（級）の惑星は赤色超巨星と呼ばれている。これらの恒星は非常に大きいので，私たちの小さな太陽系の大半がその1つの恒星の中に収まることもありうるのである。もし，太陽が赤色超巨星に変わるとしたら，太陽の大きさは木星の軌道を越えるだろう。

重要語句リスト

space	图 宇宙
lots of ~	熟 たくさんの~
form	图 形態，形
mostly	副 大半は，大部分は
be made up of ~	熟 ~から構成されている
something like ~	熟 ~のようなもの［こと］
thousands of ~	熟 何千もの~
explosion	图 爆発
close	形 近い，接近した
planet	图 惑星，地球
medium	形 中位の
size	图 大きさ
yellow dwarf	图 黄色矮星
different	形 異なる，違った
burn	動 燃える
million	图 百万
around	副 周囲に［を］
supergiant	图 超巨星
so … that S V	熟 非常に…なので，SがVする
solar system	图 太陽系
fit inside	熟 ~の中に収まる
turn into ~	熟 ~に変わる
orbit	图 軌道

❹ Stars, (just like people), have a life, but a star's life is much longer (than a human's). The sun is billions of years old and will live (for many more billions <of years>). (When our sun starts to die), it will grow (into a red giant star). It will (not) become a supergiant (because it is (not) heavy enough). (When our sun dies), it will get so hot (that the heat and light will burn the Earth. (In fact), it will be too hot (for anything <to live (on the Earth)>) (when our sun becomes a red giant). (Then), our sun will (slowly) get darker and colder (until it stops giving (off) any energy (at all)).

❹ 恒星は，ちょうど人間のように，寿命を持つが，恒星の寿命は人間のものよりずっと長い。太陽は数十億歳であり，ここからさらに数十億年も存在するだろう。太陽が消え始めるとき，それは赤色巨星へと発達するだろう。太陽は質量が十分ではないので，超巨星にはならないだろう。太陽が消えるとき，それはとても高温になるのでその熱と光は地球を燃やすだろう。実際，太陽が赤色巨星になるとき，それはあまりに高温すぎて地球上ではいかなる生物も生存できないだろう。その後，太陽は全くエネルギーを放出しなくなるまで，ゆっくりとだんだん暗く冷たくなるのである。

☐ billions of ～	熟 何十億の～
☐ die	動 消える，死ぬ
☐ grow into ～	熟 ～へと発達する，～に成長する
☐ giant	形 巨大な
☐ heavy	形 重い
☐ enough	副 十分に
☐ the Earth	名 地球
☐ in fact	熟 実際は
☐ too … for ～ to V	熟 ～にとってあまりにも…すぎて V できない
☐ slowly	副 ゆっくりと
☐ get 比較級 and 比較級	熟 だんだん～になる
☐ dark	形 暗い
☐ until S V	接 S が V するまで
☐ give off ～	熟 ～を発する

END

Lesson 15
問題文

■ Read the passage and answer the following questions.

Competition in the marketplace requires that the buyer not only knows what is good for him or her but also what is good. If the seller produces nothing of value, as determined by a rational or reasonable marketplace, then he or she loses out. It is the assumption of rationality among buyers that spurs* competitors to become winners, and winners to keep on winning. Where it is assumed that a buyer is unable to make rational or reasoned decisions, laws are passed to invalidate* transactions, as, for example, those which prohibit children from making contracts. In America, there even exists in law a requirement that sellers must tell the truth about their products, for if the buyer has no protection from false claims, rational decision-making is seriously impaired*.

The move away from the use of propositions* in commercial advertising began at the end of the nineteenth century. But it was not until the 1950's that the television commercial made linguistic discourse* obsolete* as the basis for product decisions. By substituting images for claims, the pictorial commercial made emotional appeal, not (x)tests of truth, the basis of consumer decisions. The distance between rationality and advertising is now so wide that it is difficult to remember that there once existed a connection between them. Today, on television commercials, propositions are as scarce as unattractive people. The truth or falsity of an advertiser's claim is simply not an issue. A McDonald's commercial, for example, is not a series of testable, logically ordered assertions. It is a drama — a mythology, if you will — of handsome people selling, buying and eating hamburgers, and being driven to near ecstasy by their good fortune. No claims are made, except those the viewer projects onto or infers from the drama. One can like or dislike a television commercial, of course. But one cannot refute it.

Indeed, we may go this far: The television commercial is not at all about the character of products to be consumed. It is about the character of the consumers of products. Images of movie stars and famous athletes, of serene lakes and macho fishing trips, of elegant dinners and romantic interludes[*], of happy families packing their station wagons for a picnic in the country — these tell nothing about the products being sold. But they tell everything about the fears, fancies, and dreams of those who might buy them. What the advertiser needs to know is not what is right about the product but what is wrong with the buyer. And so, the balance of business expenditures shifts from *product* research to *market* research. The television commercial has oriented business away from making products of value and toward making consumers feel valuable, which means that the business of business has now become pseudo[*]-therapy. The consumer is a patient assured by psycho-dramas.

(Source: Neil Postman, Amusing *Ourselves to Death*, Penguin Books, Viking Penguin Inc. 1984. pp.127-128)

* spur（駆り立てる）　invalidate transactions（商取引を無効にする）
  impair（損なう）　proposition（提案，意見）
  discourse（対話，談話）　obsolete（時代遅れの）
  interlude（合間（の出来事））　pseudo-（擬似的な）

Lesson 15
設問

(1) What does paragraph 1 infer about markets?

    1 They create wealth for many people.

    2 They operate in a sensible way.

    3 They make people more intelligent.

    4 They require a stable currency.

(2) In the first paragraph, the author uses the phrase "prohibit children from making contracts" in order to

    1 illustrate how young people are being wronged.

    2 suggest that parents sign contracts for children.

    3 exemplify a group that may not be fully rational.

    4 point out the need for better child labor laws.

(3) The phrase "tests of truth" in line (X) is closest in meaning to

    1 Factual analysis.

    2 Informal contests.

    3 Verifying identities.

    4 Confirming profitability.

(4) What is the main point of the third paragraph?

    1 Buyers have to become more reasonable.

    2 Too many products are making false claims.

    3 More people should actively seek out therapy.

    4 Emotions may have replaced reason in the market.

(5) With which of the following statements would the author most likely agree?

    1 Commercials often still have significant intellectual content.

    2 Only government regulations can improve current commercials.

    3 The best products in the market may not be the best-selling ones.

    4 Most smart people simply ignore common advertisements.

No.	(1)	(2)	(3)	(4)	(5)
配点	10点	10点	10点	10点	10点
解答欄					

解答用紙

Lesson 15
解答・解説

(1) 第1段落で市場について暗示していることは何か。
1 市場が多くの人たちの富を作り出している。
② 市場は賢明な方法で動いている。
3 市場は人々をより聡明にする。
4 市場は安定通貨を必要とする。

解説▶ 第1段落第2文「もし，売り手が価値のないものを生み出すと，それが合理的な道理にかなった市場によって（無価値であると）判定されるので，彼（売り手）は損をする」より，**市場は合理的，つまり，賢明に動いている**と読み取れる。よって，**2** が正解となる。

(2) 第1段落の中で，著者は……ために，「prohibit children from making contracts」という表現を用いている。
1 若者がいかに不当に取り扱われているのかを例証する
2 親が子供のための契約に署名してはどうかと提案する
③ あまり合理的ではないかもしれない集団を例示する
4 より良い児童労働法の必要性を指摘する

解説▶ 同文の前半部分より，「**買い手が合理的，また筋の通った判断をすることができないと想定される場合**」の一例として，設問箇所が挙げられていることが読み取れる。よって，**3** が正解となる。

(3) 下線部（X）の「tests of truth」という表現は，……に最も意味が近い。
① 事実にもとづく分析
2 非公式のコンテスト
3 本人であると確かめること
4 利益性を確かめること

解説▶ 「tests of truth」は「事実の分析」という意味より，**1** が正解となる。

Lesson 15 (3／5)　問題文→設問→解答・解説→構造分析

(4) 第3段落の主な要点は何か。
1　買い手はより道理をわきまえるようにならなければならない。
2　あまりに多すぎる製品が見当はずれの主張をしている。
3　より多くの人々は積極的に治療法を捜し出すべきだ。
④　感情は市場の中で理性にとって代わってしまったかもしれない。

解説▶第3段落第7文前半「テレビコマーシャルはビジネスを価値がある製品を作ることから，消費者に価値があると感じさせることへと関心を向け」より，**「価値ある製品を作る＝理性」**から**「価値があると感じさせる＝感情」**にとって変わってしまったかもしれないことが読み取れる。よって，**4** が正解となる。

(5) 著者は以下のどの記述に最も同意しそうか。
1　コマーシャルはいまだに重要で知性のある内容であることが多い。
2　政府の規制によってのみ，現在のコマーシャルは向上しうる。
③　市場での最良の製品は最もよく売れる製品ではないかもしれない。
4　大多数の賢い人たちは一般的な広告を単に無視する。

解説▶第3段落第7文前半より，市場は**「価値がある製品＝最良の製品」**を作ることから，**「消費者に価値があると感じさせる製品＝最もよく売れる製品」**に向いていることがわかる。よって，**3** が正解となる。

Lesson 15

正　解

No.	(1)	(2)	(3)	(4)	(5)
配点	10点	10点	10点	10点	10点
解答欄	**2**	**3**	**1**	**4**	**3**

| 得点 | （1回目） ／50点 | （2回目） | （3回目） | CHECK YOUR LEVEL | 0〜30点 ➡ *Work harder!*
31〜40点 ➡ *OK!*
41〜50点 ➡ *Way to go!* |

Lesson 15
構造分析

[ ]=名詞　☐=修飾される名詞　< >=形容詞・同格　( )=副詞
S=主語　V=動詞　O=目的語　C=補語　'=従節

❶ Competition <in the marketplace> requires [that the buyer (not only) knows [what is good (for him or her)] (but also) [what is good]]. (If the seller produces nothing <of value>), (as determined (by a rational or reasonable marketplace)), (then) he or she loses (out). It is the assumption <of rationality (among buyers)> that spurs competitors (to become winners), and winners (to keep (on winning)). (Where it is assumed [that a buyer is unable to make rational or reasoned decisions]), laws are passed (to invalidate transactions), (as, (for example), those <which prohibit children (from making contracts)>). (In America), there (even) exists (in law) a requirement <that sellers must tell the truth (about their products)>, for (if the buyer has no protection <from false claims>), rational decision-making is (seriously) impaired.

❷ The move <away from the use <of propositions (in commercial advertising)>> began (at the end <of the nineteenth century>). But it was not (until the 1950's) that the television commercial made linguistic discourse obsolete (as the basis <for product decisions>). (By substituting images (for claims)), the pictorial commercial made emotional appeal, not tests <of truth>, the basis <of consumer decisions>. The distance <between rationality and advertising> is (now) so wide (that it is difficult [to remember [that there once existed a connection (between them)]]). (Today), (on television commercials), propositions are as scarce (as unattractive people). The truth or falsity <of an advertiser's claim> is (simply) (not) an issue. A McDonald's commercial, (for example), is (not) a series <of testable, (logically) ordered assertions>. It is a drama — <a mythology>, (if you will) — <of handsome people selling, buying and eating hamburgers, and being driven (to

Lesson 15 (4／5)　問題文→設問→解答・解説→構造分析

【和訳】

❶ 市場における競争では，買い手は自身にとって何が良いものかを知っているだけではなく，良いものとは何かを知っていることも求められる。もし，売り手が価値のないものを生み出すと，それが合理的な道理にかなった市場によって（無価値であると）判定されるので，彼（売り手）は損をする。競争者（競争している売り手）が勝者になるように，また勝者が勝ち続けるようにと駆り立てるものは，買い手の間にある合理性という前提である。買い手が合理的，また筋の通った判断をすることができないと想定される場合，例えば，子供が契約をすることを禁止する法律のような，商取引を無効にするための法律が可決される。アメリカでは，法律の中に，もし買い手が誤った主張からの保護（自身を守る術）を持っていなければ，合理的な意思決定がひどく損なわれるため，売り手は自身の商品について真実を述べなければならないという要求さえ存在する。

❷ 商業広告における提案（の形）を用いることから離れる動きが，19世紀の終わりに始まった。しかし，1950年代になって，テレビコマーシャルは，商品を決定する土台として，言語的な対話を時代遅れなものにした。映像を（事実を）主張することの代わりに用いることで，映像のコマーシャルは，事実の分析ではなく，感情的な訴えを消費者が決断をする基準にした。合理性と広告の間の距離は今や非常に広いので，かつてはその間につながりが存在したと思い出すことは難しい。今日，テレビコマーシャルにおいて，提案（の形）は見た目がさえない人と同じほどまれである。広告主の主張の真偽は全く問題ではない。例えば，マクドナルドのコマーシャルは分析できる，論理的に整理された一連の主張ではない。それは，ハンサムな人々がハンバーガーを売り，買い，食べ，そしてその幸福によりほぼ恍惚

重要語句リスト

□ competition	名 競争
□ marketplace	名 市場
□ require	動 求める，必要とする
□ buyer	名 買い手
□ not only A but also B	熟 AばかりでなくBも
□ seller	名 売り手
□ produce	動 生み出す，作る
□ determine	動 判定する，決定する
□ rational	形 合理的な，理性的な
□ reasonable	形 道理にかなった
□ assumption	名 前提，仮定
□ keep on Ving	熟 Vし続ける
□ assume	動 想定する，当然だと思う
□ be unable to V	熟 Vできない
□ reasoned	形 筋の通った
□ decision	名 判断，決定
□ law	名 法律
□ pass	動 可決する，通り過ぎる
□ transaction	名 取引，処理
□ for example	熟 例えば
□ prohibit	動 禁止する
□ contract	名 契約
□ exist	動 存在する
□ requirement	名 要求，要件
□ truth	名 真実，事実
□ product	名 商品，産物
□ protection	名 保護
□ false	形 誤った
□ claim	名 主張
□ seriously	副 ひどく，真面目に
□ away from ~	熟 ~から離れて
□ commercial	形 商業の，営業の
□ advertising	名 広告
□ linguistic	形 言語的な，言語の
□ basis	名 基準，基礎
□ substitute A for B	熟 AをBの代わりに用いる
□ pictorial	形 映像の，絵画［写真］の
□ emotional	形 感情的な，感情の
□ appeal	名 訴えること，魅力
□ consumer	名 消費者
□ distance	名 距離
□ rationality	名 合理性
□ wide	形 広い

Lesson 15

near ecstasy) (by their good fortune)>. No claims are made, (except those <the viewer projects (onto) or infers (from the drama)>). One can like or dislike a television commercial, (of course). But one can (not) refute it.

❸ (Indeed), we may go (this far): The television commercial is (not) (at all) (about the character <of products <to be consumed>>). It is (about the character <of the consumers <of products>>). Images <of movie stars and famous athletes>, <of serene lakes and macho fishing trips>, <of elegant dinners and romantic interludes>, <of happy families packing their station wagons (for a picnic) (in the country)> — these tell nothing <about the products being sold>. But they tell everything <about the fears, fancies, and dreams <of those <who might buy them>>>. [What the advertiser needs to know] is (not) [what is right (about the product)] but [what is wrong (with the buyer)]. And (so), the balance <of business expenditures> shifts (from *product* research) (to *market* research). The television commercial has oriented business (away from making products <of value>) and (toward making consumers feel valuable), which means [that the business <of business> has (now) become pseudo-therapy]. The consumer is a patient <assured (by psycho-dramas)>.

164

状態にされるドラマであり，言うなれば神話である。視聴者がそのドラマに対して投げかけたり，それから推測したりするものを除けば，主張は何もなされていない。もちろん，人は（誰でも）テレビコマーシャルには好き嫌いがある。しかし，否定することはできない。

❸ 実際，我々はここまでするかもしれない。テレビコマーシャルは消費される製品の特徴についてでは全くない。それは製品の消費者の特徴についてである。映画スターや有名なアスリート，澄み渡った湖や男らしい釣り旅行，優雅な夕飯やロマンチックな合間のできごと，楽しそうな家族が田舎でのピクニックのためにステーションワゴンに荷物を詰めている映像，これらは売られている製品については何も語っていない。しかし，それら（映像）はそれら（製品）を買うかもしれない人々の不安，好み，夢についてのすべてを語っている。広告主が知る必要があることは，製品について何が正しいのかではなく，買い手について何が問題であるのかである。そこで，商経費のバランスは「製品」調査から「市場」調査へと変わっている。テレビコマーシャルはビジネスを価値がある製品を作ることから，消費者に価値があると感じさせることへと関心を向け，それは，ビジネスの本分が今や擬似的な治療となったことを意味する。消費者は，心理劇療法によって安心させられる患者なのである。

☐ unattractive	形 見た目がさえない，魅力のない
☐ falsity	名 虚偽，誤り
☐ simply	副 全く，単に
☐ issue	名 問題
☐ testable	形 分析できる，検証できる
☐ logically	副 論理的に，必然的に
☐ assertion	名 主張
☐ mythology	名 神話
☐ handsome	形 ハンサムな，美しい
☐ ecstasy	名 恍惚，歓喜
☐ fortune	名 幸運
☐ except	前 〜を除いて
☐ viewer	名 視聴者
☐ project	動 投射する
☐ infer from 〜	熟 〜から推測する
☐ dislike	動 嫌う
☐ refute	動 否定する，間違いを証明する
☐ indeed	副 実際に，本当に
☐ far	副 さらに，はるかに
☐ character	名 特徴，登場人物
☐ athlete	名 アスリート，運動選手
☐ macho	形 男らしさをひけらかす
☐ serene	形 澄み渡った
☐ elegant	形 優雅な
☐ romantic	形 ロマンチックな，恋愛に関する
☐ pack	動 詰め込む
☐ station wagon	名 ステーションワゴン
☐ fear	名 不安，恐怖，恐れ
☐ fancy	名 好み，空想，想像
☐ advertiser	名 広告主
☐ balance	名 バランス，釣り合い
☐ expenditure	名 経費
☐ orient	動 関心を向ける
☐ assure	動 安心させる，保証する
☐ psycho-drama	名 心理劇療法

END

Special Column（生徒から東進講師陣に質問！）

Please teach me, teacher!

Q 4技能試験のリーディングの問題文は，何に注意しながら読んでいけばいいんですか？

A 一般的に，英検やTOEFL，TEAPなどという4技能試験の素材は，「アカデミック」な題材から選ばれています。こうした文章は，一般的に「評論文」や「論説文」と呼ばれています。筆者の体験を語り，その経験にもとづいて得られたことを述べるエッセイ文や，架空の人物が登場する物語文と比べて，上記に挙げられた評論文（論説文）は，資格試験だけではなく，様々な英語力を問う試験の問題として扱われています。

評論文（論説文）を読むときに注意することはいくつかありますが，その中で最も大切なことは，「パラグラフ」の意識をしっかり持っておくということです。パラグラフとは日本語の「段落」にあたる言葉ですが，英語の評論文では，このパラグラフの役割を非常に大切にします。

一般的に，英語の評論文では，「伝えたいメッセージは1つのパラグラフに1つだけ」と決まっています。そのため皆さんは，本書に掲載されている長文をいきなり読むのではなくて，最初にパラグラフをつけるというところから始めるようにしましょう。また，せっかくパラグラフをつけるのですから，そのパラグラフでどのようなことが伝えたいのかということを読みながら短くメモを取るような意識を持つとよいでしょう。パラグラフの内容を軽くまとめておくことで話の内容が整理しやすくなりますし，設問で問われている内容がどのあたりに書かれていたかということが探しやすいというメリットもあります。

もう1つ，評論文（論説文）を読むときに知っておくと便利なのは，Discourse Markersと呼ばれる語(句)を活用して，話の流れを大きく把握していくことです。Discourse Markersとは，「しかし」や「従って」のような話の流れを論理的につなげる語(句)のことです。先程の「しかし」は英語ではhowever，「従って」はthereforeです。このような論理的に文と文をつなげる役割をする語をうまく活用することによって，大きな文章の筋道がわかることもあるのです。

（回答：東進英語科講師）

Premium Reading Workbook

Standard
STAGE-4
Lesson 16 – 20

The University of Chicago is a world-class institution of higher education. Its mission is to produce a caliber of teaching and research that regularly leads to advances in fields such as medicine, biology, physics, economics, critical theory and public policy. Our Facilities Services' team supports that mission through efforts to maintain and enhance the University campus and environment and provide superior client service to our community including faculty, students, staff, neighbors and visitors.

The University of Chicago

Lesson 16
問題文

■ Read the passage and answer the following questions.

　In the past, taking a course in a second foreign language, such as French or German, made one feel like a full-fledged* university student reaching out for something (1) English, which was the only foreign language required in high school. But times are changing. In fact, some universities are (2) the second language requirement.

　An acquaintance who teaches Spanish at a private university in Tokyo told me that each year he notices more and more students don't own a dictionary. He recommends several dictionaries at the start of the course, but when he asked his class during the third lesson this year how many had (3) his advice, only three among the 30 students answered that they had purchased a dictionary. It used to be common sense for anyone studying a foreign language to purchase at least one dictionary. For today's students, the main reasons cited for not getting a dictionary are said to be: "too expensive," "too heavy to carry around" and "too much of a bother to look words up."

　A veteran instructor at another private university recounted* an (4) that took place 10 years ago. When he permitted his students to bring dictionaries to a French-to-Japanese translation test he was giving, one student brought not only a French-Japanese dictionary, but also a Japanese dictionary. The student explained he needed the (5) one to make sure his Japanese translations were perfect. This kind of episode is history.

　The foreign-languages section of any bookstore today is crammed* with copies of flimsy* books bearing titles that promise (6) languages in a matter of days. Not surprisingly, these books skip grammar. But they are snapped up* by students who don't buy dictionaries.

　Perhaps it is not "cool" today to even attempt to read a foreign language book (7) a dictionary. But patient effort is basic to becoming proficient* in a foreign language, and this truism will never change.

* full-fledged（一人前の）　　recount（詳しく話す）　　cram（ぎっしり詰める）
　flimsy（薄っぺらな）　　snap up（先を争って買う）　　proficient（堪能な）

Lesson 16
設問

Choose the best word or phrase from among the four choices to fill each gap.

(1) **1** insofar as **2** beyond
    3 whatever **4** if only

(2) **1** doing away with **2** getting in line to
    3 setting out for **4** pulling up

(3) **1** reserved **2** confused
    3 followed **4** substituted

(4) **1** orientation **2** illustration
    3 acclimation **4** episode

(5) **1** latter **2** terminal
    3 dependent **4** rearmost

(6) **1** dexterity in **2** convenience of
    3 no-sweat mastery of **4** imagination through

(7) **1** as allowed by **2** in response to
    3 in tune with **4** with the aid of

解 答 用 紙

No.	(1)	(2)	(3)	(4)	(5)	(6)	(7)
配点	5点	5点	5点	5点	10点	10点	10点
解答欄							

Lesson 16
解答・解説

(1) 1 〜する限りにおいて　　② 〜以上に
　　　3 どんな〜でも　　　　　4 〜しさえすれば

解説 ▶「以前は，フランス語やドイツ語のような第二外国語のコースをとることは，英語，これは高校で求められる唯一の外国語であるのだが，これ（ 1 ）何かを知的に手を伸ばして取ろうとする一人前の大学生のような感じがした」が文意。大学生は，英語までしか学べなかった高校時代よりも，**より幅広く学問を修めるために，第二外国語を学んでいた**ことが読み取れる。よって，**2** が正解と判断できる。

(2) ① 〜を廃止している　　　2 列に並んでいる
　　　3 〜に向けて出発している　4 止めている

解説 ▶「実際，第二外国語の必修を（ 2 ）大学もある」が文意。第1段落第2文「しかし，時代は変化している」より，**大学生が必ずしも第二外国語を学ぶわけではなくなっている**ことが読み取れる。よって，**1** が正解と判断できる。**4** の pull up は目的語に人や車を指す名詞をとるので，不適切。

(3) 1 予約していた　　　　　2 困惑させていた
　　　③ 従っていた　　　　　　4 代わりに用いていた

解説 ▶「彼は，コースの初めにいくつかの辞書を勧めるが，彼がその年の第3回目の授業の中で彼のクラスの学生に，何名が彼のアドバイスに（ 3 ）かを尋ねると，30名のうちたった3名だけが辞書を購入したと答えた」が文意。3名だけが辞書を買った，すなわち彼のアドバイスを聞いたということが読み取れる。よって，**3** が正解と判断できる。

(4) 1 オリエンテーション　　　2 実例
　　　3 順応　　　　　　　　　　④ エピソード

解説 ▶「別の私立大学のベテラン指導者は10年前に起きた（ 4 ）について詳しく述べた」が文意。第3段落最終文「**この種のエピソードは過去のことである**」と述べられていることから，**4** が正解とわかる。

(5) ①　後者の　　　　　　　　② 終末の
　　 ③　頼っている　　　　　　④ 最後の

解説▶「その学生は，彼の日本語の翻訳が完璧なものかを確かめるために（５）が必要であると説明した」が文意。直前の第3段落第2文では「彼が学生に与えたフランス語から日本語への翻訳テストで，辞書の持ち込みを許したとき，ある学生は仏和辞書だけではなく，日本語の辞書も持ってきた」と述べられており，日本語の翻訳が完璧なものかを確かめるのに使用するのは日本語の辞書であることがわかる。よって，**1** が正解。

(6) １　～における器用さ　　　　２ ～の便利さ
　　 ③　～の汗をかかない熟達　　④ ～を通じた想像

解説▶「今日，いかなる本屋でも外国語のセクションは，ほんの数日のうちに言語（６）を約束するタイトルを冠する何冊もの薄っぺらな本でぎっしり詰められている」が文意。辞書を引くといった**手間をかけずに言語を上達させようとしている人が増えている状況**が読み取れる。よって，**3** が正解。

(7) １　～によって許された　　　　２ ～への返答で
　　 ３　～とかみ合って　　　　　　④ ～の助けを借りて

解説▶「おそらく，辞書（７）外国語の本を読もうと試みることでさえ『クール（かっこいいこと）』ではないのかもしれない」が文意。直前の第4段落では**手間をかけない言語の熟達を謳う本が人気を博している状況**が述べられていることから，辞書を使って言語を地道に学ぶことはマイナスイメージを帯びてきていることが読み取れる。よって，**4** が正解。

正解

No.	(1)	(2)	(3)	(4)	(5)	(6)	(7)
配点	5点	5点	5点	5点	10点	10点	10点
解答欄	**2**	**1**	**3**	**4**	**1**	**3**	**4**

得点	(1回目) /50点	(2回目)	(3回目)	CHECK YOUR LEVEL	0～30点 ➡ Work harder! 31～40点 ➡ OK! 41～50点 ➡ Way to go!

Lesson 16
構造分析

[ ]＝名詞　　▢＝修飾される名詞　　< >＝形容詞・同格　　( )＝副詞
S＝主語　V＝動詞　O＝目的語　C＝補語　′＝従節

❶ (In the past), [taking a course <in a second foreign language>], <such as French or German>, made one feel (like a full-fledged university student <reaching (out) (for something <beyond English>)>), (which was the only foreign language <required (in high school)>). But times are changing. (In fact), some universities are doing (away) (with the second language requirement).

❷ An acquaintance <who teaches Spanish (at a private university) (in Tokyo)> told me [that (each year) he notices [more and more students don't own a dictionary]]. He recommends several dictionaries (at the start <of the course>), but (when he asked his class (during the third lesson <this year>) [how many had followed his advice]), only three <among the 30 students> answered [that they had purchased a dictionary]. It used to be common sense (for anyone <studying a foreign language>) [to purchase (at least) one dictionary]. (For today's students), the main reasons <cited (for not getting a dictionary)> are said to be: "too expensive," "too heavy (to carry around)" and "too much <of a bother> (to look words up)."

❸ A veteran instructor <at another private university> recounted an episode <that took place (10 years ago)>. (When he permitted his students (to bring dictionaries (to a French-to-Japanese translation test <he was giving>))), one student brought (not only) a French-Japanese dictionary, (but also) a Japanese dictionary. The student explained [he needed the latter one (to make sure [his Japanese translations were perfect])]. This kind <of episode> is history.

Lesson 16 (4/5) 問題文→設問→解答・解説→構造分析

【和訳】

❶ 以前は，フランス語やドイツ語のような第二外国語のコースをとることは，英語，これは高校で求められる唯一の外国語であるのだが，これ以上の何かを知的に手を伸ばして取ろうとする一人前の大学生のような感じがした。しかし，時代は変化している。実際，第二外国語の必修を廃止している大学もある。

❷ 東京の私立大学でスペイン語を教えている知人は私に，ますます多くの学生が辞書を所有していないことに毎年気づくと話した。彼は，コースの初めにいくつかの辞書を勧めるが，彼がその年の第3回目の授業の中で彼のクラスの学生に，何名が彼のアドバイスに従っていたかを尋ねると，30名のうちたった3名だけが辞書を購入したと答えた。少なくとも1つの辞書を購入するのは，外国語を勉強する者にとっては，かつては常識であった。今日の学生にとって，辞書を手に入れないことに対して引き合いに出される主な理由は，「高すぎる」，「持ち運ぶには重すぎる」，「単語を調べるのは面倒」というものであると言われている。

❸ 別の私立大学のベテラン指導者は10年前に起きたエピソードについて詳しく述べた。彼が学生に与えたフランス語から日本語への翻訳テストで，辞書の持ち込みを許したとき，ある学生は仏和辞書だけではなく，日本語の辞書も持ってきた。その学生は，彼の日本語の翻訳が完璧なものかを確かめるために後者（日本語の辞書）が必要であると説明した。この種のエピソードは過去のことである。

重要語句リスト

□ reach out for ~	熟	手を伸ばして~を取ろうとする
□ beyond	前	~以上に，~を越えて
□ require	動	求める，必要とする
□ do away with ~	熟	~を廃止する
□ requirement	名	要求，要件
□ acquaintance	名	知人
□ private	形	私立の，個人的な
□ notice	動	気づく
□ more and more S V	熟	ますます多くのSがVする
□ recommend	動	勧める
□ purchase	動	購入する，買い物をする
□ used to V	熟	かつてはVだった，Vするのが常だった
□ common sense	名	常識
□ at least ~	熟	少なくとも~
□ cite	動	引き合いに出す
□ expensive	形	高価な
□ carry	動	運ぶ
□ bother	名	面倒
□ look ~ up	熟	~を調べる
□ veteran	形	ベテランの
□ instructor	名	指導者，教師
□ episode	名	エピソード
□ take place	熟	起こる，行われる
□ permit	動	許す，許可する
□ translation	名	翻訳
□ not only A but also B		AばかりでなくBも（熟）
□ explain	動	説明する
□ make sure S V	熟	SがVするのを確かめる

Lesson 16

❹ The foreign-languages section <of any bookstore (today)> is crammed (with copies <of flimsy books <bearing titles <that promise no-sweat mastery <of languages> (in a matter <of days>)>>>). (Not surprisingly), these books skip grammar. But they are snapped (up) (by students <who do(n't) buy dictionaries>).

❺ (Perhaps) it is (not) "cool" (today) [to (even) attempt to read a foreign language book (with the aid <of a dictionary>)]. But patient effort is basic (to [becoming proficient (in a foreign language)]), and this truism will (never) change.

❹ 今日，いかなる本屋でも外国語のセクションは，ほんの数日のうちに言語の汗をかかない（苦労せず）熟達を約束するタイトルを冠する何冊もの薄っぺらな本でぎっしり詰められている。驚くことではないが，これらの本は文法を省いている。しかし，それらは辞書を買わない学生に先を争うように買われている。

❺ おそらく，辞書の助けを借りて外国語の本を読もうと試みることでさえ「クール（かっこいいこと）」ではないのかもしれない。しかし，忍耐強い努力は，外国語に堪能になることにおいて基本であり，このわかりきったことは決して変わることはないのであろう。

☐ copy	名 冊，写し
☐ bear	動 持つ
☐ promise	動 約束する
☐ mastery	名 熟達
☐ a matter of ~	熟 ほんのわずかな~
☐ not surprisingly	熟 驚くことではないが
☐ skip	動 省く，抜かす
☐ grammar	名 文法
☐ attempt	動 試みる
☐ aid	名 助け，援助

Lesson 17
問題文

Read the passage and answer the following questions.

One of the key human characteristics is our tendency to act to help others by sharing resources such as money and food with people in need, or comforting people in distress. It is often assumed that such altruistic* behaviors are cultural in origin. Our parents taught us moral standards or rewarded us for being nice to others. However, research findings suggest that human altruism has deeper roots than previously thought.

Young children are eager to find out why people do what they do. When one-year-olds watch someone use a novel tool, or press buttons on fancy pieces of equipment that create a surprising effect, they can tell what the person did purposefully and what he or she did accidentally. When it is the child's turn to use the tool or press the buttons, the child does not copy everything the person did but only what the person intended to do. Children are intention reader, not just behavior copier.

Then, would young children use their intention-reading capacity not only for their own ends but also to help others? In one study, eighteen-month-old children observed a researcher performing an action when suddenly a problem occurred that prevented him from achieving his goal. The children helped the researcher spontaneously without being asked or being praised for their efforts. They picked up clothespins* the researcher had dropped on the ground and was unsuccessfully reaching for. They opened the doors of a cabinet when the experimenter bumped into it while carrying a stack of magazines he was trying to put inside. It is important to note that those children did not perform these behaviors when the same basic situation was established but with no indication that it presented a problem for the researcher.

During another experiment, half of the children received a reward for helping and the other half did not. Subsequently, the children again had the opportunity to help but now without a reward being offered to either group. The results showed that the children who had been rewarded initially were no more likely to help spontaneously than the children who had not been rewarded. This conclusion suggests that children's behavior of helping others is innately* motivated rather than driven by the expectation of material reward.

Children determined whether help was needed or not, exhibiting sophisticated intention-reading capacities. The fact that this behavior emerges so early in children's lives is important, because it suggests that the social rules and morality of one's culture are not the original source of altruistic behavior in humans.

* altruistic（利他的な）　clothespin（洗濯バサミ）
  innately（生まれながらに）

Lesson 17
設問

(1) What is the topic of the paragraph that most likely preceded this passage?

    1 Common features in a personality

    2 Difficulties in raising children

    3 Selecting proper exam procedures

    4 Punishments and incentives

(2) According to the passage, one purpose of children's intention-reading is to

    1 see if one can succeed in a task.

    2 understand the rules of a test.

    3 improve the mastery of a technology.

    4 determine which actions to duplicate.

(3) The author suggests that offering rewards for altruism will most likely

    1 excessively increase research costs.

    2 skew the results of an experiment.

    3 have little effect on outcomes.

    4 reduce the level of spontaneity.

(4) The author organizes the discussion according to what principle?
  1 A comparison of multiple theories on a phenomenon
  2 An assertion that is empirically substantiated
  3 An introduction and criticism of a dominant concept
  4 A question that is raised but then left open for analysis

No.	(1)	(2)	(3)	(4)
配点	10点	10点	10点	20点
解答欄				

解答用紙

Lesson 17
解答・解説

(1) この文章の前に最もありそうな段落のトピックは何か。
- **①** 性格の一般的な特徴
- **2** 子供を育てていくときに困ったこと
- **3** 適切な試験手順を選ぶこと
- **4** 罰と動機

解説▶ 導入文である第1段落第1文「人間の重要な特性の1つは，お金や食料のような資源を困っている人々と共有したり，窮地にいる人々を慰めたりと，他者を助けるための行動をする傾向があることである」に注目。「the」は通常，既出の情報に用いられる。文頭の「one of the key human characteristics」に注目すると，「the key human characteristics」が既出の情報，つまりこの段落以前で述べられていたと推測できる。よって，**1**が正解と判断できる。

(2) 本文によると，子供が意図を読み取る1つの目的は……ためだ。
- **1** 誰かがある任務に成功しうるかどうかを見る
- **2** ある試験のルールを理解する
- **3** ある技術の熟達を改善する
- **④** 真似をする行動を発見する

解説▶ 子供が意図を読み取る内容に関しては，第2段落で述べられている。第4文に「子供は単に行動を真似るのではなく，意図を読み取っているのである」とあるが，直前の第3文では「子供はその人がしたことをすべて真似るのではなく，その人がしようとしたことだけを真似る」とされている。つまり，**子供は意図を読み取ることで，特定の行動のみを真似る**（＝真似をする行動を発見する）ことがわかる。よって，**4**が正解と判断できる。

(3) 筆者は，利他主義への報酬を提供することは最もよく……であろうことを示している。
- **1** 過度に研究費用を増加させる
- **2** ある実験の結果をゆがめる
- **③** ほとんど結果への影響はない
- **4** 自発性の程度を減少させる

解説▶ 報酬に関する実験は，第4段落で述べられている。最終文「他者を助けるという子供の行動は，物理的な報酬への期待によって駆り立てられるというよりも，生まれつき動機づけされていると示される」より，

利他主義は生まれながらのものであり，報酬によって結果が変わるものではないことが読み取れる。よって，**3** が正解と判断できる。

(4) 筆者が議論を構成するのに従っている原則は何か。
   1 ある現象についての複数の理論の比較
   ② 実験によって実証された主張
   3 主要な概念の導入と批評
   4 提起されているが，その後分析されないままにされている問題

   解説▶本文は筆者の考えと，その考えを実証するための実験内容で構成されていることに着目する。第2段落最終文「子供は単に行動を真似るのでなく，意図を読み取っているのである」という考えは，第2段落第2～3文で述べられている実験によって，裏付けられている。また，第4段落最終文「他者を助けるという子供の行動は，物質的な報酬への期待によって駆り立てられるというよりも，生まれつき動機づけされている」という考えは，第4段落第1～3文で述べられている実験によって裏付けられており，**筆者の主張は一貫して実験を根拠にしている**ことが読み取れる。よって，**2** が正解と判断できる。

	正　解			
No.	(1)	(2)	(3)	(4)
配点	10点	10点	10点	20点
解答欄	**1**	**4**	**3**	**2**

得点　(1回目)　／50点　(2回目)　(3回目)　CHECK YOUR LEVEL　0～30点 ➡ *Work harder!*　31～40点 ➡ *OK!*　41～50点 ➡ *Way to go!*

Lesson 17
構造分析

[ ]=名詞　□=修飾される名詞　< >=形容詞・同格　( )=副詞
S=主語　V=動詞　O=目的語　C=補語　'=従節

❶ [One] <of the key human characteristics> is [our tendency] <to act (to help others) (by sharing [resources] <such as money and food> (with [people] <in need>), or comforting [people] <in distress>)>. It is (often) assumed [that such altruistic behaviors are cultural (in origin)]. Our parents taught us moral standards or rewarded us (for being nice (to others)). (However), research findings suggest [that human altruism has deeper roots (than previously thought)].

❷ Young children are eager to find (out) [why people do [what they do]]. (When one-year-olds watch [someone] <use a novel tool>, or <press [buttons] <on [fancy pieces of equipment] <that create a surprising effect>>>), they can tell [what the person did (purposefully)] and [what he or she did (accidentally)]. (When it is [the child's turn] <to use the tool or press the buttons>), the child does (not) copy [everything] <the person did> but only [what the person intended to do]. Children are intention reader, (not) (just) behavior copier.

Lesson 17 (4/5) 問題文→設問→解答・解説→構造分析

【和訳】

❶ 人間の重要な特性の1つは、お金や食料のような資源を困っている人々と共有したり、窮地にいる人々を慰めたりと、他者を助けるための行動をする傾向があることである。そのような利他的な行動は、もとは文化的なものを発端とするとしばしば想定される。両親が（私たちに）道徳的な基準を教え、（私たちが）他者に対して親切にすると（両親は）褒美をくれた。しかし、研究における発見により、人間の利他主義は以前に考えられていたよりも深い根源を持っているかもしれないと示されている。

❷ 幼児は、なぜ（ほかの）人々がある行動をとるのか理解したいと思っている。1歳児は、誰かが新しい道具を使うのを見たり、びっくりさせる効果を生み出す一風変わった装置のボタンを押すのを見るとき、その人が意図を持ってしたことと、偶然したことをわかっている。子供がその道具を使ったりボタンを押したりする番になったとき、子供はその人がしたことをすべて真似るのではなく、その人がしようとしたことだけを真似る。子供は単に行動を真似るのでなく、意図を読み取っているのである。

重要語句リスト

☐ one of ~	熟 ~の1つ
☐ key	形 重要な
☐ human	形 人間の
☐ characteristic	名 特性、登場人物
☐ tendency to V	熟 ~する傾向
☐ act	動 行動する
☐ share	動 共有する、分け合う
☐ resource	名 資源、資産
☐ A such as B	熟 BのようなA
☐ in need	熟 困っている、必要として
☐ comfort	動 慰める
☐ people in distress	熟 窮地にいる人、困窮している人
☐ assume	動 想定する、当然だと思う
☐ behavior	名 行動、ふるまい
☐ in origin	熟 もとは
☐ reward	動 褒美を与える
☐ however	副 しかしながら
☐ finding	名 発見、成果、結論
☐ suggest	動 示す、提案する
☐ root	名 根源、根本
☐ previously	副 以前に
☐ be eager to V	熟 Vしたいと思う
☐ find out ~	熟 ~を理解する、見つけ出す
☐ what S V	熟 SがVすること
☐ novel	形 新しい、斬新な
☐ fancy	形 変わった
☐ pieces of ~	熟 いくつかの~
☐ equipment	名 装置
☐ surprising	形 びっくりさせるような、驚くような
☐ purposefully	副 意図的に
☐ accidentally	副 偶然に
☐ turn	名 順番
☐ copy	動 真似をする
☐ intend to V	熟 Vしようとする
☐ intention	名 意図
☐ copier	名 真似する人

Lesson 17

❸ (Then), would young children use their intention-reading capacity (not only for their own ends) (but also to help others)? (In one study), eighteen-month-old children observed a researcher <performing an action> (when (suddenly) a problem occurred <that prevented him (from achieving his goal)>). The children helped the researcher (spontaneously) (without being asked or being praised (for their efforts)). They picked (up) clothespins <the researcher had dropped (on the ground) and was (unsuccessfully) reaching for>. They opened the doors <of a cabinet> (when the experimenter bumped (into it) (while carrying a stack of magazines <he was trying to put (inside)>)). It is important [to note [that those children did (not) perform these behaviors (when the same basic situation was established but with no indication <that it presented a problem <for the researcher>>)]].

❹ (During another experiment), half <of the children> received a reward (for helping) and the other half did (not). (Subsequently), the children (again) had the opportunity <to help> but (now) (without a reward <being offered (to either group)>). The results showed [that the children <who had been rewarded (initially)> were (no more) likely to help (spontaneously) (than the children <who had (not) been rewarded>)]. This conclusion suggests [that children's behavior <of helping others> is (innately) motivated (rather than driven (by the expectation <of material reward>))].

❺ Children determined [whether help was needed or not], (exhibiting sophisticated intention-reading capacities). The fact <that this behavior emerges (so early) (in children's lives)> is important, (because it suggests [that the social rules and morality <of one's culture> are (not) the original source <of altruistic behavior <in humans>>]).

❸ では，幼児は意図を読み取る能力を自分自身の目的のためだけでなく，他者を助けるためにも使うのだろうか。ある研究では，18ヵ月の子供は，研究者の目的達成を妨げる問題が突然起こったとき，研究者が（その目的達成のための）行動をしているのを見た。その子供たちは，頼まれたり，努力を褒められたりしなくても，自発的に研究者を助けた。彼らは，研究者が地面に落とし，うまく手が届かなかった洗濯ばさみを拾った。また，実験者が戸棚の中に入れようとしている雑誌の山を持って，戸棚にぶつかったときドアを開いてあげた。そうした子供たちが，同じような基本的な状況が確立されても，それが研究者にとって問題であるというしるしがないときは，こうした行動を見せなかった，というのは注目に値する。

❹ 別の実験では，子供たちの半分は（他者を）助けることで褒美を受け取り，もう半分は受け取らなかった。その後，子供たちは再び他者を助ける機会があったが，今回はどちらの集団に対しても褒美が与えられなかった。その結果は，最初に褒美を与えられた子供たちは，褒美を与えられなかった子供たちと同じように自発的には助けようとはしなかった。この結論により，他者を助けるという子供の行動は，物質的な報酬への期待によって駆り立てられるというよりも，生まれつき動機づけされていると示される。

❺ 子供は助けが必要かどうかを判断しており，そのことは（子供の）意図を読み取る洗練された能力を示している。この行動が非常に幼い頃から現れるという事実は重要である。というのも，その事実は，文化の社会的な規則や道徳が，人間の利他的な行動の起源ではないということを示しているからである。

☐ capacity	名	能力
☐ not only A but also B	熟	AばかりでなくBも
☐ study	名	研究，調査
☐ observe	動	気づく，観察する
☐ perform	動	行う，遂行する
☐ occur	動	起こる，生じる
☐ prevent ~ from Ving	熟	~がVするのを妨げる
☐ achieve	動	達成する
☐ goal	名	目的，目標
☐ spontaneously	副	自発的に
☐ praise	動	褒める，賞賛する
☐ pick up ~	熟	~を拾う
☐ drop	動	落とす，落ちる
☐ unsuccessfully	副	うまくいかずに
☐ reach for ~	熟	~に届く
☐ cabinet	名	戸棚
☐ experimenter	名	実験者
☐ bump into ~	熟	~にぶつかる，~に偶然出くわす
☐ carry	動	運ぶ
☐ a stack of ~	熟	~の山
☐ try to V	熟	Vしようと試みる
☐ note	動	注目する，気づく
☐ establish	動	確立する，築き上げる
☐ indication	名	しるし，徴候
☐ present	動	見せる，提示する
☐ half of ~	熟	半分の~
☐ subsequently	副	その後，次に
☐ offer	動	与える，提案する
☐ initially	副	最初に，はじめに
☐ be likely to V	熟	Vする傾向にある，しそうである
☐ conclusion	名	結論
☐ motivate	動	動機づける
☐ determine	動	判断する，決定する
☐ whether A or B	接	AかBか，AであろうがBであろうが
☐ exhibit	動	示す
☐ sophisticated	形	洗練された
☐ emerge	動	現れる
☐ rule	名	規則
☐ morality	名	道徳，道徳性
☐ original	形	最初の

END

Lesson 18
問題文

■ Read the passage and answer the following questions.

It is surprising that the basic pattern of our three daily meals — breakfast, lunch and dinner — has been established only since 1890. It is the result of a development through many centuries.

Meal times have been different in various countries and eras. They are the outcome of many circumstances such as climate, occupations and general working conditions.

Originally, Anglo-Saxon* tradition knew of only two meals a day — breakfast and dinner. In the 16th century, breakfast was a snack*, with no fixed menu. Its only purpose was to *break one's fast*. But 200 years later it had become a larger meal; not just for the family, but for plenty of guests as well. It was a social occasion for the upper class, which started at 10 a.m. and often lasted till 1 p.m. Then breakfast began to decline. It became relatively small and was taken at a much earlier hour. By 1850 it had retreated to 8 a.m. and shrunk to a family affair.

Dinner, however, (x)went the other way. In the 16th century it was eaten at 11 a.m. Years afterward, it moved to the early afternoon, then to 5 p.m. By 1850 it had reached 7 p.m. or 8 p.m.

Lunch is a relatively recent introduction. It first appeared on the time-table as a snack to fill the gap between breakfast and dinner. In his Dictionary of 1755, Dr. Johnson defined it as "As much food as one's hand can hold."

The original meaning of lunch maintains its early frugality.* It means a *lump* — a piece of whatever you may choose to swallow. As breakfast became ever earlier and dinner later, lunch assumed an important position and developed into a big meal. The division of the working day in the Victorian age into two periods — from 9 a.m. to 1 p.m. and from 2 p.m. to 6 p.m. — finally made lunch an institution.

That is how the three daily meals, as they are known today, came into being. It is quite possible that, with ever shorter working hours, lack of domestic help, concern for diets and the popularity of prepared dishes, the pattern and rhythm of our meal times will change again.

* Anglo-Saxon（アングロサクソン族，今日の英国人の主な祖先）
  snack（軽食）　　break one's fast（断食をやめる）　　frugality（質素さ）

Lesson 18
設問

(1) What is the main purpose of the passage?

　　1 To develop a statistical trend

　　2 To historicize a phenomenon

　　3 To compare various alternatives

　　4 To analyze multiple theories

(2) The phrase "went the other way" in line (X) is closest in meaning to

　　1 stopped an ongoing challenge.

　　2 travelled quickly downward.

　　3 changed in an opposite way.

　　4 remained out of view.

(3) According to the passage, a consequence of a change in the Victorian working day was

　　1 an early breakfast.　　**2** a substantial lunch.

　　3 a two-meal system.　　**4** an omission of dinner.

(4) With which of the following statements would the author most likely agree?

1 Food has become unhealthy.

2 Meals have become much bigger.

3 Governments have overregulated meals.

4 Dietary patterns adapt to different eras.

(5) What will the paragraph immediately following this passage most likely discuss?

1 Future lifestyles and dining

2 Sustainable farming patterns

3 Restaurant ownership laws

4 Survival cooking skills

解 答 用 紙					
No.	(1)	(2)	(3)	(4)	(5)
配点	10点	10点	10点	10点	10点
解答欄					

Lesson 18
解答・解説

(1) 本文の主な目的は何か。
1 統計に見られる動きを発展させるため　**2** 現象を歴史化するため
3 様々な代替手段を比較するため　4 複数の理論を分析するため

解説▶ 本文は「朝食・昼食・夕食という，我々の1日3食という基本的な様式は1890年から確立されたにすぎないというのは驚きである」という導入で始まり，続く段落以降では，**1日3食の様式に至るまでの食事の様式の変遷**について述べられている。よって，**2**が正解と判断できる。

(2) 下線部(X)の「went the other way」という表現は，……と最も意味が近い。
1 進行中の挑戦をやめた　　　2 すばやく下部へ伝わった
3 逆の方向に変わった　　　4 視界の外にとどまった

解説▶ 「しかしながら，夕食は went the other way」が文意。文頭のHowever（しかしながら）に注目。この表現は，基本的に前後で逆の内容を接続するときに用いられる。前段落では，**朝食をとる時間がどんどん早まっていった**ことが述べられている。一方で，下線部を含む文以降では，**夕食をとる時間がどんどん遅くなった**ことが述べられている。つまり，下線部は「逆であった」の意味で用いられていることがわかる。よって，**3**が正解。また，「the other way」の直訳は「逆方向」である。

(3) 本文によると，ビクトリア朝時代の労働日の変化がもたらす結果は……であった。
1 早めの朝食　　　　　　**2** たくさんの昼食
3 1日2食方式　　　　　　4 夕食の省略

解説▶ 第6段落第3～4文「朝食がますます早くなり，夕食が遅くなるにつれて，昼食は重要な立場を引き受け，大きな（量がある）食事へと発展した。ビクトリア朝において，労働を，午前9時から午後1時と，午後2時から午後6時の2つの時間帯に分ける区分により，最終的に昼食が慣習となった」と述べられている。第3段落最終文「1850年までには，それは午前8時まで時間が早くなり，……」，第4段落最終文「1850年までに，それは午後7時もしくは午後8時になった」より，第6段落で述べられていた昼食の発展は1850年までに，つまりビクトリア朝時代に起きていたことが読み取れる。よって，**2**が正解と判断できる。

(4) 筆者が最も同意しそうなのは以下の陳述のどれか。
 1　食糧は不健康なものとなった。
 2　食事はずっと大規模なものとなった。
 3　政府は過剰な食事規制をした。
 ④　食事の様式は異なる時代に順応する。

　解説▶第7段落最終文「労働時間がますます短くなり，家事を手伝うことに欠け，食品に関する関心や調理済み食品の人気のために，我々の食事回数についての様式や周期が再び変わることは十分ありうる」と述べられていることから，食事の様式は時代の変化とともに変わりゆく可能性があることが読み取れる。よって，**4** が正解と判断できる。

(5) 本文の直後に続く段落において最も議論しそうなことは何か。
 ①　将来の生活様式と食事　　　2　持続可能な農業様式
 3　レストラン所有の法律　　　4　生き残るための料理の技術

　解説▶本文は1日3食の様式に至るまでの食事の様式の変遷について述べ，第7段落最終文「労働時間がますます短くなり，家事を手伝うことに欠け，食品に関する関心や調理済み食品の人気のために，我々の食事回数についての様式や周期が再び変わることは十分にありうる」と締められている。つまり，続く段落では将来の食事の様式がどう変化するかについて述べられるだろうと予測できる。よって，**1** が正解とわかる。

	正　解				
No.	(1)	(2)	(3)	(4)	(5)
配点	10点	10点	10点	10点	10点
解答欄	**2**	**3**	**2**	**4**	**1**

得点	(1回目) /50点	(2回目)	(3回目)	CHECK YOUR LEVEL	0～30点 ➡ Work harder! 31～40点 ➡ OK! 41～50点 ➡ Way to go!

Lesson 18

Lesson 18
構造分析

[　]=名詞　　□=修飾される名詞　　< >=形容詞・同格　　( )=副詞
S=主語　V=動詞　O=目的語　C=補語　'=従節

❶ It is surprising [that [the basic pattern] <of our three daily meals> ― breakfast, lunch and dinner ― > has been established (only since 1890)]. It is [the result] <of [a development] <through many centuries>>.

❷ [Meal times] have been different (in various countries and eras). They are [the outcome] <of [many circumstances] <such as climate, occupations and general working conditions>>.

❸ (Originally), Anglo-Saxon tradition knew (of only two meals (a day)) <― breakfast and dinner>. (In the 16th century), breakfast was a snack, (with no fixed menu). Its only purpose was [to *break one's fast*]. But (200 years later) it had become a larger meal; (not) (just) (for the family), but (for [plenty] <of guests> (as well)). It was [a social occasion] <for the upper class>, (which started (at 10 a.m.) and (often) lasted (till 1 p.m.)) (Then) breakfast began to decline. It became relatively small and was taken (at a much earlier hour). (By 1850) it had retreated (to 8 a.m.) and shrunk (to a family affair).

❹ Dinner, (however), went (the other way). (In the 16th century) it was eaten (at 11 a.m.) (Years afterward), it moved (to the early afternoon), (then) (to 5 p.m.) (By 1850) it had reached 7 p.m. or 8 p.m.

❺ Lunch is a relatively recent introduction. It (first) appeared (on the timetable) (as a snack) (to fill [the gap] <between breakfast and dinner>). (In [his Dictionary] <of 1755>), Dr. Johnson defined it (as "As much food (as one's hand can hold))."

Lesson 18 (4/5)　問題文→設問→解答・解説→構造分析

【和訳】

❶ 朝食・昼食・夕食という，我々の1日3食という基本的な様式は1890年から確立されたにすぎないというのは驚きである。それは何世紀も通しての発展の結果であるのだ。

❷ 食事の回数は，様々な国や時代で異なってきた。それらは，気候，職業，一般的な労働状況など多くの状況の結果なのである。

❸ 元来，アングロサクソン族の慣習は1日たった2食であるとわかっている。朝食と夕食である。16世紀は，朝食は，決まったメニューのない軽食であった。その（朝食の）唯一の目的は「断食をやめる」ことであった。しかし，200年後，それ（朝食）は，より規模が大きい食事となり，家族のためだけではなく，多くのゲストのためのものにもなった。それは，上流階級にとっての社交の場であり，午前10時に始まり，しばしば午後1時まで続いた。その後，朝食は衰退し始めた。それは比較的，小規模なものになり，はるかに早い時間にとられるようになった。1850年までには，それは午前8時まで時間が早くなり，家族で行うことにまで規模を縮小した。

❹ しかしながら，夕食は逆であった。16世紀は，それは午前11時に食べられていた。数年後，それは午後の早い時間へと移動し，そして午後5時になった。1850年までに，それは午後7時もしくは午後8時になった。

❺ 昼食は比較的最近導入されたものである。それは，最初は予定の上で，朝食と夕食の間のギャップを埋めるための軽食として現れた。1755年の辞書で，Johnson博士はそれ（昼食）を「片手で持てるだけの量」として定義していた。

重要語句リスト

It is surprising that S V	熟 SがVするとは驚きだ
basic	形 基本的な
pattern	名 様式，傾向
establish	動 確立する，築き上げる
result	名 結果
development	名 発展，発達
various	形 様々な
era	名 時代
outcome	名 結果，成果
circumstance	名 状況
climate	名 気候
occupation	名 職業，従事すること
general	形 一般的な，一般の
working	形 労働の，労働に従事する
condition	名 状況，状態
originally	副 元来
tradition	名 慣習，伝統
snack	名 軽食
fixed	形 決まった，不変の
purpose	名 目的
plenty of ～	熟 多くの～
guest	名 ゲスト，客
occasion	名 機会，場合
upper	形 上部の
class	名 階級
last	動 続く
decline	動 衰退する，断る
relatively	副 比較的
retreat	動 後退する
shrink	動 縮小する
affair	名 事柄
afterward	副 その後
move	動 移動する，動かせる
reach	動 達する
introduction	名 導入
appear	動 現れる
fill	動 満たす，いっぱいになる
gap	名 ギャップ，切れ目
define	動 定義する，明らかにする

❻ The original meaning <of lunch> maintains its early frugality. It means a lump <— a piece <of [whatever you may choose to swallow]>>. (As breakfast became ever earlier and dinner later), lunch assumed an important position and developed (into a big meal). The division <of the working day <in the Victorian age>> <into two periods> <— (from 9 a.m.) (to 1 p.m.) and (from 2 p.m.) (to 6 p.m.) —> (finally) made lunch an institution.

❼ That is [how the three daily meals, (as they are known today), came (into being)]. It is quite possible [that, (with ever shorter working hours, lack <of domestic help>, concern <for diets> and the popularity <of prepared dishes>), the pattern and rhythm <of our meal times> will change (again)].

❻ 昼食の元来の意味は，その初期の質素さを主張している。それは，lump（小さな塊）を意味しており，それは，どんなものであれ飲み込もうとするもののひとかけらである。朝食がますます早くなり，夕食が遅くなるにつれて，昼食は重要な立場を引き受け，大きな（量がある）食事へと発展した。ビクトリア朝において，労働を，午前9時から午後1時と，午後2時から午後6時の2つの時間帯に分ける区分により，最終的に昼食が慣習となった。

❼ そのようにして，今日我々が知る，1日3食が実現した。労働時間がますます短くなり，家事を手伝うことに欠け，食品に関する関心や調理済み食品の人気のために，我々の食事回数についての様式や周期が再び変わることは十分にありうる。

☐ maintain	動 主張する，維持する
☐ choose	動 選ぶ
☐ swallow	動 飲み込む
☐ assume	動 引き受ける，想定する
☐ position	名 立場，位置
☐ division	名 区分，分裂，分配
☐ institution	名 慣習，制度
☐ domestic	形 家庭の，国内の
☐ concern	名 関心（事），懸念
☐ popularity	名 人気
☐ prepared dish	名 調理済み食品
☐ rhythm	名 周期

Lesson 19
問題文

単語数 ▶ 406 words
制限時間 ▶ 20 分
目標得点 ▶ 40 / 50点

DATE

■ **Read the passage and answer the following questions.**

　It is now almost exactly two centuries since the first two of English author Jane Austen's* novels — *Sense and Sensibility* and *Pride and Prejudice* — were published. The particular genius and lasting appeal of Austen's writing has only become clearer and more certain as the decades pass and literary fashions come and go. What is Austen's particular genius? And what might explain the renewed popular interest in her work today — one reflected in the many recent and much-praised television and film productions of her books?

　There are a number of reasons why Austen's books have not only endured but grown in popularity. Her delightful wit is certainly one of the great pleasures of her work. As for her style of writing, it is precise and full of intelligence. But it may be said that Austen's greatest talent lies in her deep understanding of human nature. We can still, despite the very great differences between her society and our own, recognize ourselves in the ways her characters think and behave. And though times have certainly changed over the past 200 years, still today it is our own nature and actions, and the nature and actions of the people around us, that most influence our lives.

　In fact, it is often noted that Austen's sensibilities are very similar to today's sensibilities. Unlike the writers who were in fashion during her time but are now long forgotten, she did not hesitate to portray ordinary life as it really was. Her heroines, for example, are not simply pure and good, but more complicated, with unique and often sparkling personalities. As for relationships between men and women, her stories show love and romance to be limited by economic circumstances and human imperfection. Readers today are great fans of Austen's strong heroines, girls and women who think for themselves and say what they mean, who do not take themselves too seriously. We are as interested as ever in Austen's favorite subjects of love and marriage, and appreciate her refusal to idealize romance: her recognition that money, class, and what other people think do matter even when we are in love; that marriage does not result in a happy ending for everyone; and that it is dangerous to let passion make us blind to reality. What is more, readers appreciate Austen's emphasis on reason, loyalty, and consideration for others, values that are still as important today as they were two centuries ago.

(The Penguin Reading Guides to Pride and Prejudice, http://us.penguingroup.com/static/rguides/us/pride_and_prejudice.html, 改変有)

＊　Jane Austen（ジェイン・オースティン (1775 – 1817) は英国の小説家。代表作は『プライドと偏見』）

Lesson 19
設問

(1) According to paragraph 2, all of the following are stated as reasons for Jane Austen's continuing popularity EXCEPT

   1 Publishers have marketed the books more widely.

   2 The works contain an appealing type of humor.

   3 Her characters are recognizable to people of today.

   4 Her comprehension of nature of humanity was accurate.

(2) The phrase "great pleasures" in the passage refers to the belief that

   1 It is wonderful that authors can develop their wits.

   2 Readers have the opportunity to enjoy special styles.

   3 Books are more widely available than they previously were.

   4 Intelligent people can understand writers' intentions better.

(3) How does paragraph 3 relate to the earlier discussion of human nature?

　1 It shows why important ideas were overlooked.

　2 It suggests that a fixed pattern was quickly changed.

　3 It provides an opposing theory for a long-term trend.

　4 It goes into detail on a topic that was introduced.

(4) According to paragraph 3, Jane Austen would most likely agree with which of the following statements?

　1 True love can overcome any difficult circumstance.

　2 People should follow their passions no matter what.

　3 Others' opinions influence personal actions.

　4 Happy marriages often derive from idealizing romance.

No.	(1)	(2)	(3)	(4)
配点	10点	10点	10点	20点
解答欄				

Lesson 19
解答・解説

(1) 第2段落によると，……を除く以下のすべてがジェイン・オースティンの継続する人気の理由として述べられている。
　① 出版社はより広範囲にわたって本を売り出している。
　2 作品は魅力的なユーモアの一種を含んでいる。
　3 彼女の（作品における）登場人物は今日の人々に認識できるものだ。
　4 人間の本質についての彼女の理解は的確だった。
　解説▶ **2** は第2文「彼女の人を愉快にさせるウイットは，確かに作品の大きな楽しみの1つである」，**3** は第5文「…我々はいまだに彼女の（作品における）登場人物が考え行動する方法で，自分自身を認識することができる」，**4** は第4文「しかし，オースティンの最も偉大な才能は，人間の本質を深く理解していることにあると言えるかもしれない」でそれぞれ述べられている。よって **1** が正解とわかる。

(2) 本文の「great pleasures」の表現は……という考えに言及している。
　1 筆者が自らのウイットを向上させることができるのはすばらしいことだ。
　② 読者は特別なスタイルを楽しむ機会がある。
　3 本は以前よりもより広範囲に渡って入手できる。
　4 聡明な人々は作家の意図をよりよく理解できる。
　解説▶ 問題の表現は第2段落第2文に見られる。「彼女の人を愉快にさせるウイットは，確かに作品の大きな楽しみの1つである」が文意。「great pleasure」の表現により，彼女のウイットによって愉快な気分になること，つまり，彼女のウイットを理解することで，より深く作品を楽しめることがオースティンの作品の魅力であると読み取れる。よって **2** が正解とわかる。

(3) 第3段落は人間の本質についての以前の議論とどのように関係があるか。
1 それはなぜ重要な考えが見落とされていたのかを示している。
2 それは定着した様式がすぐに変化したことを示している。
3 それは長期の傾向に相反する理論を与えている。
④ それは導入されたトピックについて詳しく述べている。

解説▶第2段落では，第5文「彼女が生きた社会と我々自身の社会には，大きな違いがあるにもかかわらず，我々はいまだに彼女の（作品における）登場人物が考え行動する方法で，自分自身を認識することができる」と，人間の本質に関するオースティンの洞察についてのトピックが導入されている。続く第3段落では，「実際，オースティンの感性は今日の感性と非常に似ているとしばしば指摘されている」という導入で始まり，具体例を挙げながら，オースティンの洞察について詳細が述べられている。よって，**4**が正解と判断できる。

(4) 第3段落によると，ジェイン・オースティンが最も同意しそうなのは以下の陳述のどれか。
1 真実の愛はあらゆる困難な状況に打ち勝つことができる。
2 人々はどんな感情であっても，自身の感情に従うべきだ。
③ ほかの人々の意見は個人の行動に影響する。
4 幸せな結婚はしばしば恋愛を理想化することから得られる。

解説▶第6文に「2人が愛し合っているときでさえ，お金，階級，ほかの人々の考えは非常に重要であるという認識であり」と述べられている。よって**3**が正解とわかる。

正　解

No.	(1)	(2)	(3)	(4)
配点	10点	10点	10点	20点
解答欄	**1**	**2**	**4**	**3**

得点　(1回目) /50点　(2回目)　(3回目)
CHECK YOUR LEVEL　0〜30点 ➡ Work harder!　31〜40点 ➡ OK!　41〜50点 ➡ Way to go!

Lesson 19
構造分析

[　] = 名詞　　□ = 修飾される名詞　　< > = 形容詞・同格　　( ) = 副詞
S = 主語　V = 動詞　O = 目的語　C = 補語　' = 従節

❶ It is (now) almost exactly two centuries (since [the first two] <of English author Jane Austen's novels — *Sense and Sensibility* and *Pride and Prejudice* — > were published). [The particular genius and lasting appeal] <of Austen's writing> has (only) become clearer and more certain (as the decades pass and literary fashions come and go). What is Austen's particular genius? And what might explain [the renewed popular interest] <in her work today> — [one] <reflected (in [the many recent and much-praised television and film productions] <of her books>)>?

❷ There are [a number of reasons] <why Austen's books have (not only) endured but grown (in popularity)>. Her delightful wit is (certainly) [one] <of [the great pleasures] <of her work>>. (As for [her style] <of writing>), it is precise and full (of intelligence). But it may be said [that Austen's greatest talent lies (in [her deep understanding] <of human nature>)]. We can (still), (despite [the very great differences] <between her society and our own>), recognize ourselves (in [the ways] <her characters think and behave>). And (though times have (certainly) changed (over the past 200 years)), (still) (today) it is our own nature and actions, and [the nature and actions] <of [the people] <around us>>, [that (most) influence our lives].

【和訳】

❶ 英国の作家であるジェイン・オースティンの最初の2つの小説――『分別と多感（Sense and Sensibility）』と『プライドと偏見（Pride and Prejudice）』――が出版されてから，現在ほぼ2世紀が経った。（出版から）何十年も経ち，文学的な流行り廃りがある中で，オースティンの作品の格別な才能と長く続く魅力は，より明確で疑いのないものになってきている。オースティンの格別な才能とは何だろうか。また最近になって，非常に賞賛されている彼女の本に関する多くのテレビ番組や映画作品に反映されているように，今日，彼女の作品に対する民衆の新しい関心を説明しうるものは何であろうか。

❷ オースティンの本（の人気）が持ちこたえているだけでなく，人気も高まっていることに対する多くの理由がある。彼女の人を愉快にさせるウイットは，確かに作品の大きな楽しみの1つである。彼女の執筆スタイルに関して言えば，それは正確で知性にあふれている。しかし，オースティンの最も偉大な才能は，人間の本質を深く理解していることにあると言えるかもしれない。彼女が生きた社会と我々自身の社会には，大きな違いがあるにもかかわらず，我々はいまだに彼女の（作品における）登場人物が考え行動する方法で，自分自身を認識することができる。また，ここ200年で，時代は確実に変化してきたが，今日でも，我々の生活に最も影響を与えるのは，我々自身の性質や行動，また周囲の人間たちの性質や行動である。

重要語句リスト

□ almost exactly	熟	ほぼ正確に
□ author	名	作家，筆者
□ novel	名	小説
□ publish	動	出版する
□ particular	形	格別の
□ genius	名	才能，天才
□ lasting	形	長く続く，永続する
□ appeal	名	魅力，訴えること
□ certain	形	疑いのない，特定の
□ decade	名	10年間
□ pass	動	（時間が）経つ，過ごす
□ literary	形	文学の
□ explain	動	説明する
□ renewed interest	名	新しい関心，よみがえった興味
□ reflect	動	反映する，反射する
□ recent	形	最近の
□ praise	動	賞賛する，褒める
□ production	名	作品，制作
□ a number of ~	熟	多くの~
□ endure	動	持続する，我慢する
□ grow in popularity	熟	人気が高まる
□ delightful	形	人を愉快にさせる
□ wit	名	ウイット，ユーモア
□ certainly	副	確かに
□ pleasure	名	楽しさ，喜び
□ work	名	作品，研究
□ as for ~	熟	~に関して言えば
□ precise	形	正確な
□ intelligence	名	知性
□ it is said that S V		SがVすると言われている
□ talent	名	才能
□ lie in ~	熟	~にある
□ nature	名	本質，性質
□ despite	前	~にもかかわらず
□ recognize	動	認識する
□ behave	動	行動する，ふるまう

❸ (In fact), it is (often) noted [that Austen's sensibilities are very similar (to today's sensibilities)]. (Unlike the writers <who were (in fashion) (during her time) but are (now) (long) forgotten>), she did (not) hesitate (to portray ordinary life) (as it really was). Her heroines, (for example), are (not simply) pure and good, but more complicated, (with unique and often sparkling personalities). (As for relationships <between men and women>), her stories show love and romance (to be limited (by economic circumstances and human imperfection)). Readers (today) are great fans <of Austen's strong heroines>, girls and women <who think (for themselves) and say [what they mean]>, <who do (not) take themselves (too seriously)>. We are as interested (as ever in Austen's favorite subjects <of love and marriage>), and appreciate her refusal <to idealize romance>: her recognition <that money, class, and [what other people think] (do) matter (even) (when we are in love)>; <that marriage does (not) result (in a happy ending <for everyone>)>; and <that it is dangerous [to let passion make us blind (to reality)]>. (what is more), readers appreciate Austen's emphasis <on reason, loyalty, and consideration <for others>>, values <that are (still) as important (today) (as they were two centuries ago)>.

❸ 実際，オースティンの感性は今日の感性と非常に似ているとしばしば指摘されている。彼女の時代には流行していたが，今は久しく忘れ去られてしまった作家たちとは違って，彼女はありふれた生活をありのままに描くことをためらわなかった。例えば，彼女の小説の中のヒロインは，単に純粋で心が優しいだけでなく，より複雑で独特な，しばしば異彩を放つ個性を持っていた。男女の関係について言えば，彼女の小説は，恋愛が経済的状況や人間の欠点によって制限されると示している。今日の読者は，オースティンの小説に登場する力強いヒロインの大ファンであり，このヒロインは自主性があり，自分が言おうとすることを発言し，あまり真面目になりすぎない少女や女性なのである。我々は，愛や結婚といったオースティンのお気に入りのテーマに今までと変わらず興味を持っており，また恋愛を理想化することを彼女が拒絶していることを評価している。（恋愛を理想化することの拒絶とは）２人が愛し合っているときでさえ，お金，階級，ほかの人々の考えは非常に重要であるという認識であり，結婚は皆にとって幸せな結末になるとは限らないという認識であり，情熱に身をゆだねて，現実が見えなくなることは危険であるという認識である。さらに，読者は，オースティンが理性や忠誠心や他人への思いやり，すなわち２世紀前と同様にいまだに重要である価値観を重視していることを評価している。

☐ note	動 指摘する，気づく
☐ sensibility	名 感性
☐ similar to ～	熟 ～に似ている
☐ unlike	前 ～と違って
☐ in fashion	熟 流行している
☐ hesitate to V	熟 Vすることをためらう
☐ portray	動 描く
☐ ordinary	形 ありふれた，一般の
☐ complicated	形 複雑な
☐ sparkling	形 異彩を放つ，才気あふれる
☐ personality	名 個性，人格
☐ relationship	名 関係
☐ circumstance	名 状況
☐ imperfection	名 欠点
☐ think for oneself	熟 自主性のある
☐ mean	動 言おうとする，意味する
☐ seriously	副 真面目に，ひどく
☐ subject	名 テーマ
☐ appreciate	動 評価する
☐ refusal to V	熟 Vすることの拒絶
☐ idealize	動 理想化する
☐ class	名 階級
☐ result in ～	熟 ～という結果に終わる
☐ passion	名 情熱
☐ blind	形 目の見えない
☐ reason	名 理性
☐ loyalty	名 忠誠（心），誠実さ
☐ consideration	名 思いやり

Lesson 20
問題文

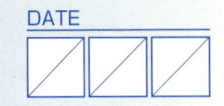

■ Read the passage and answer the following questions.

　A new study has shown that houses in areas rich with bird life sell for an average of £21,000* more than those with fewer birds. The research, which attempted to compensate for factors such as house size, age and levels of urbanisation, found that the presence of even just one uncommon species of bird was an indication of higher house prices. The (1) species there were, the higher the prices became, the researchers found. It suggests that house-hunters would do well to listen out for the sound of woodpeckers and nightingales to gauge the quality of a neighbourhood.

　The researchers also found that nearby parks did little to influence the number of birds, meaning their presence was due to nearby domestic gardens in the area. Michael Farmer, from the Department of Agricultural and Applied Economics at Texas Tech University in Lubbock who led the research, which is published in the *Journal of Urban Ecosystems*, said: 'The addition of another desirable, less ubiquitous bird species improves mean home price by £21,000. This is likely (2) the human-created landscapes on private properties immediately surrounding a home sale'.

　Bird song is already known to have a number of benefits (3) helping people to relax. One study in Liverpool found it could help calm young patients as they received injections in a hospital. The National

Trust also suggests people listen to birdsong for a few minutes each day to help (4) their mood.

Miles Shipside, a housing analyst and commercial director at property specialists Rightmove, said the relationship between property prices and birds could be explained by the value home owners place on having a garden.

He said: 'Birds are very sensitive to their environment and it could be a sign of an area having good quality gardens. This would be reflected in the property prices. But in the UK particularly, people do also put a high value on wildlife, so an area where we can see it and be close to it would be more (5)'.

(Adapted from The Daily Telegraph, 7th June, 2013, http://www.telegraph.co.uk/property/propertynews/)

* £21,000 約300万円（£〔ポンド〕はイギリスの通貨単位）

Lesson 20
設問

Choose the best word or phrase from among the four choices to fill each gap.

(1) **1** many   **2** more
     3 good   **4** better

(2) **1** for fear of   **2** for the sake of
     3 due to   **4** in case of

(3) **1** such as   **2** despite
     3 without   **4** because

(4) **1** repeat   **2** improve
     3 imitate   **4** predict

(5) **1** plain   **2** capable
     3 surprised   **4** desirable

解 答 用 紙

No.	(1)	(2)	(3)	(4)	(5)
配点	10点	10点	10点	10点	10点
解答欄					

Lesson 20
解答・解説

(1) **1** 多くの　　　**②** より多くの
　　 3 良い　　　　**4** より良い

　解説▶第1段落第1文「鳥が多い地域の家は，鳥が少ない地域より，平均して約300万円ほど高い値で売れている」から，本文は**鳥の数と家の価格は相関する**という研究内容を示す文章と考えることができる。よって，「(1)種類の鳥がいればいるほど値段が高くなるということにも研究者は気づいた」は「**より多くの**」となる **2** が正解となる。「The 比較級 $S_1 V_1$, the 比較級 $S_2 V_2$」は，「…に S_1 が V_1 すればするほど，…に S_2 は V_2 する」という意味。

(2) **1** 〜をしないように　　**2** 〜を目的として
　　 ③ 〜が原因で　　　　　**4** 〜の場合は

　解説▶「これは売られる家のすぐ近くの私有地に，人間が作り出した風景(2)のようだ」が文意。This の直前の文で「平凡な家の値が約300万円高くなる」とあり，This 以降は，売られる家の近くで人間が行ったことが書かれているので，値段が上がる理由と考えられる。つまり，**This の前文が結果，This から始まる文が原因**だとわかる。よって，**3** が正解となる。

(3) **①** 例えば〜のような　　**2** 〜にもかかわらず
　　 3 〜なしに　　　　　　**4** なぜなら〜だから

　解説▶直前に「多くの恩恵」とあり，空所(3)直後では「人をリラックスさせる」，つまり，どのような恩恵があるのかの一例を述べていることがわかる。よって，具体例を述べる **1** が正解となる。

(4) 1 繰り返す　　　　　　　　② 良くする
　　 3 真似る　　　　　　　　　4 予言する

解説 ▶ 第3段落第1文「鳥のさえずりが…多くの恩恵を持っているということはすでに知られている」より，この段落は「鳥のさえずりが人にもたらすプラス面」を述べていると想定できる。よって，「ナショナル・トラストは，気分を（ 4 ）ために鳥のさえずりを毎日数分聞くことを提案している」は，**気分をプラスにするためにという内容になると判断できる**ため，**2** が正解となる。

(5) 1 明白な　　　　　　　　　2 有能な
　　 3 驚いた　　　　　　　　　④ 望ましい

解説 ▶ 「特にイギリスでは，人々は野生生物にも高い価値を置いているため，それを見ることができ，近づくことができる場所がより（ 5 ）のだろう」が文意。つまり，**「野生生物を高く評価しているため，それらが見られる・近づける場所に価値を見出す」**という内容になると判断できる。よって，**4** が正解となる。

正　解					
No.	(1)	(2)	(3)	(4)	(5)
配点	10点	10点	10点	10点	10点
解答欄	**2**	**3**	**1**	**2**	**4**

得点	(1回目) /50点	(2回目)	(3回目)	CHECK YOUR LEVEL	0〜30点 ➡ *Work harder!* 31〜40点 ➡ *OK!* 41〜50点 ➡ *Way to go!*

Lesson 20
構造分析

[　]=名詞　　□=修飾される名詞　　< >=形容詞・同格　　(　)=副詞
S=主語　V=動詞　O=目的語　C=補語　'=従節

❶ A new study has shown [that houses <in areas <rich (with bird life)>> sell (for an average <of £21,000> more) (than those <with fewer birds>)]. The research, (which attempted to compensate (for factors <such as house size, age and levels <of urbanisation>>)), found [that the presence <of even just one uncommon species <of bird>> was an indication <of higher house prices>]. [The more species there were, the higher the prices became], the researchers found. It suggests [that house-hunters would do (well) to listen (out) (for the sound <of woodpeckers and nightingales>) (to gauge the quality <of a neighbourhood>)].

❷ The researchers (also) found [that nearby parks did little <to influence the number <of birds>>, (meaning their presence was due (to nearby domestic gardens <in the area>))]. Michael Farmer, (from the Department <of Agricultural and Applied Economics> (at Texas Tech University) (in Lubbock) <who led the research>, (which is published (in the *Journal of Urban Ecosystems*)), said: 'The addition <of another desirable, less ubiquitous bird species> improves mean home price (by £21,000). This is (likely) due (to the human-created landscapes <on private properties> <immediately surrounding a home sale>)'.

❸ Bird song is (already) known to have a number <of benefits> <such as helping people to relax>>. One study <in Liverpool> found [it could help calm young patients (as they received injections (in a hospital))]. The National Trust (also) suggests [people listen (to birdsong) (for a few minutes (each day)) (to help improve their mood)].

214

【和訳】

❶ 鳥が多い地域の家は，鳥が少ない地域より，平均して約300万円ほど高い値で売れているとあらたな研究は示している。その研究は，家の大きさ，築年数，そして都市化の程度といった要素を補おうとしたものだったが，たった1匹の珍しい種の鳥の存在でさえ，家の値段を高くするしるしであることがわかった。より多くの種類の鳥がいればいるほど値段が高くなるということにも研究者は気づいた。これは，家を探す人は地域の質を判断するためにキツツキやサヨナキドリの声によく耳を澄ますのがよいということを示している。

❷ 研究者はまた，近くの公園は鳥の数にほとんど影響を与えておらず，そしてそのことは，鳥の存在はその地区内の近くにある家庭の庭が原因であることを意味するとわかった。Journal of Urban Ecosystemsに掲載されたその研究を指揮する，ラボックにあるテキサス工科大学の農業・応用経済学部出身のMichael Farmerは（次のように）述べた。「人に好まれて，それほどありきたりではない鳥の種がもう一種増えることにより，平凡な家の値が約300万円高くなる。これは売られる家のすぐ近くの私有地に，人間が作り出した風景が原因のようだ。」と。

❸ 鳥のさえずりが，人をリラックスさせるといった多くの恩恵を持っているということはすでに知られている。リバプールでのある研究は，病院で注射を受けるとき，それ（鳥のさえずり）は幼い患者を落ち着かせることを明らかにした。また，ナショナル・トラストは，気分を良くするために鳥のさえずりを毎日数分聞くことを提案している。

重要語句リスト

study	名 研究，調査
an average of ～	熟 平均して～
more than ～	熟 ～より多い
fewer	形 少ない，少数の
research	名 研究
attempt to V	熟 Vしようと試みる
compensate for ～	熟 ～を補う，～の埋め合わせをする
factor	名 要素，要因
A such as B	熟 BのようなA
level	名 程度，度合い
urbanisation	名 都市化
presence	名 存在
even	副 ～でさえ
uncommon	形 珍しい，めったにない
species	名 種
indication	名 しるし，徴候
price	名 値段
The 比較級 $S_1 V_1$, the 比較級 $S_2 V_2$.	熟 …にS_1がV_1すればするほど，…にS_2はV_2する。
researcher	名 研究者，調査員
suggest	動 示す，提案する
house-hunter	名 家を探す人
listen out for ～	熟 ～に耳を澄ます
woodpecker	名 キツツキ
nightingale	名 サヨナキドリ
gauge	動 判断する
quality	名 (品)質
neighborhood	名 地域，地域の人々
nearby	形 近くの
do little to V	熟 ほとんどVすることがない
influence	動 影響を与える
the number of A	熟 Aの数
mean	動 意味する，言おうとする
due to ～	熟 ～が原因で，～のため
domestic	形 家庭の，国内の
garden	名 庭
department	名 学部，部門，学科
agricultural	形 農業の
applied	形 応用の
economics	名 経済学
publish	動 掲載する
journal	名 専門(雑)誌，雑誌
urban	形 都会の，都市部の
ecosystem	名 生態系

Lesson 20

❹ Miles Shipside, <a housing analyst and commercial director <at property specialists Rightmove>>, said [the relationship <between property prices and birds> could be explained (by the value <home owners place (on having a garden)>)].

❺ He said: 'Birds are very sensitive (to their environment) and it could be a sign <of an area having good quality gardens>. This would be reflected (in the property prices). But (in the UK particularly), people (do) (also) put a high value (on wildlife), so an area <where we can see it and be close (to it)> would be more desirable'.

❹ 住宅分析家であり，不動産専門のライトムーブ社の営業部長である Miles Shipside は不動産価格と鳥の関係性は，家主が庭を持つことに置く価値によって説明されるだろうと述べた。

❺ 彼は「鳥は環境に対してとても敏感で，それはその地域に良質の庭があるというしるしになりうる。これは不動産の価値にも反映されるだろう。しかし，特にイギリスでは，人々は野生生物にも高い価値を置いているため，それを見ることができ，近づくことができる場所がより望ましいのだろう。」と述べた。

☐ addition	图 増加，追加
☐ desirable	形 望ましい
☐ ubiquitous	形 至るところにある
☐ improve	動 向上させる，改善する
☐ likely	副 おそらく
☐ landscape	图 風景，景観
☐ private	形 私有の，個人的な
☐ property	图 土地，特性
☐ immediately	副 すぐに，即座に
☐ surround	動 囲む
☐ a number of ～	熟 多数の～
☐ benefit	图 恩恵，利益
☐ relax	動 リラックスする，くつろぐ
☐ calm	動 落ち着かせる
☐ receive	動 受ける，受け取る
☐ injection	图 注射
☐ bird song	图 鳥のさえずり
☐ analyst	图 分析家
☐ commercial	形 営業の，商業の
☐ director	图 部長，製作責任者，管理者
☐ specialist	图 専門家
☐ relationship	图 関係，結び付き
☐ between A and B	熟 AとBの間
☐ explain	動 説明する
☐ value	图 価値
☐ owner	图 所有主
☐ sensitive	形 敏感な
☐ sign	图 しるし，合図
☐ reflect	動 反映する，反射する
☐ particularly	副 特に
☐ wildlife	图 野生生物

END

Special Column（生徒から東進講師陣に質問！）

Please teach me, teacher!

Q 制限時間内に長文問題を解き終えるために，気をつけるべきことはありますか。

A 制限時間内に長文問題を解き終わらない，そのポイントは3つあります。まず，このような質問をするということは，すらすら読みたい英文と自分の実力の間に大きなギャップがあると思われます。まずは学校や予備校の先生たちが教えてくれることを忠実に学び，単語力，文法力，構文把握力などの「知識」をきちんとつけることです。

　そして，この「知識」がついたあとには，英文を読みながら色々考えることが多くなるので，長文を読むスピードが遅くなります。2つ目のポイントはここです。このせいで一瞬スランプに陥った感じがあるのですが，ここが実は，さらなる実力をつけるチャンス！　同じ英文を何度も読んで，すらすら読めるようになるまで繰り返しましょう。すらすら読めると気持ちいいですよ。最初はわからない単語が気になるでしょうから，読んでいく中でおおまかな意味を覚えてください。次に，英文構造が難しくてつまってしまうでしょうから，どういう構造なのかを確認して，その文を何度も読んで意味を理解します。そうしているうちにすらすら読めるようになります。

　最後のポイントは，これはほとんどの人にあてはまると思うのですが，「問題を解くのが遅い」ために制限時間内に解けない，ということです。意外なことですが，制限時間内に解くコツと英文を読む速さは，あまり関係がありません。どちらかというと，「英文を読む時間を短くする」よりも，「設問を処理する時間を短くする」ことを考えましょう。訳す必要もない問題なのに選択肢を日本語に訳して考えてみたり，頭を使って英文の意味を考えずにはじめから消去法を使うなど，思いあたる部分があるのではないでしょうか？　単に「英文の該当部分と選択肢を比べるだけ」という頭を使わずに解ける問題もたくさんあります。無駄な作業を減らすことで，設問を処理する時間は短くなります。自分の解答方法で無駄な部分がないか，しっかり考えてください。

（回答：東進英語科講師）

出典一覧

LIST OF SOURCES

Level	Stage	Lesson No.	出典（著作物名）	出題大学
Standard	STAGE-1	01	Reading & Vocabulary Development 4 : Concepts & Comments, Third	東海大学
		02	Conventions and underlying stories by Rob Schwartz	拓殖大学
		03	（大学独自作成）	南山大学
		04	Man vs. Wild : Survival Techniques from the Most Dangerous Places on Earth	福岡大学
		05	Baby Talk	東洋大学
	STAGE-2	06	Heartbreak hurts people physically, too	富山大学
		07	The Undercover Scientist : Investigating the Mishaps of Everyday Life	東京慈恵会医科大学
		08	Controlling anger before it controls you	信州大学
		09	Pet subject inspires some big thinking	津田塾大学
		10	（大学独自作成）	大東文化大学
	STAGE-3	11	（出典不明）	創価大学
		12	The History and Lost Art of Letter Writing	日本女子大学
		13	The Five-Minute Linguist	岩手大学
		14	Reading for Speed and Fluency 4	近畿大学
		15	Amusing Ourselves to Death	自治医科大学
	STAGE-4	16	College kids too 'cool' for bilingual dictionaries	明治大学
		17	Future Science : Essays from the Cutting Edge	関東学院大学
		18	How Did It Begin : Customs, superstitions and their romantic origins	東洋大学
		19	PENGUINCLASSICS.COM Reading Guides 'Sense and Sensibility'	日本女子大学
		20	Birds in the neighbourhood may mean higher house prices	岐阜大学
Advanced	STAGE-1	01	The Geography of Thought: How Asians and Westerners Think Differently	法政大学
		02	Taking Medicine, With a Microchip Under the Skin	東京理科大学
		03	Community Gardens May Produce More than Vegetables	神戸大学
		04	50 Facts That Should Change The World	慶應義塾大学
		05	（大学独自作成）	南山大学
	STAGE-2	06	How to Slice a Cake Fairly	東京理科大学
		07	How to Study Television	青山学院大学
		08	Stolz, Amerikaner zu sein	広島大学
		09	What is the History of Eyeglasses?	学習院女子大学
		10	Baby Gap-How to Boost Birthrates and Avoid Demographic Decline	九州大学
	STAGE-3	11	"communication." Compton's by Britannica. Britannica Online for Kids.	関西学院大学
		12	Safe Passage for Salmon?	和歌山県立医科大学
		13	What I Wish I Knew When I Was 20	関西学院大学
		14	What Are Friends For? A Longer Life	学習院大学
		15	The Invisible Gorilla: How Our Intuitions Deceive Us	中央大学
	STAGE-4	16	The Bilingual Brain Is Sharper and More Focused, Study Says	早稲田大学
		17	Why We Cooperate	慶應義塾大学
		18	Campbell Biology: Global Edition, 9/E	横浜市立大学
		19	A website to combat bullying　The Japan Times	上智大学
		20	Everything Is Obvious: How Common Sense Fails Us	法政大学
Top	STAGE-1	01	Don't Sleep, There Are Snakes : Life and Language in the Amazonian Jungle	神戸大学
		02	Inside of a Dog: What Dogs See, Smell, and Know	神戸大学
		03	Zoosemiotics : Proposals for a Handbook	青山学院大学
		04	Star Struck	関西学院大学
		05	The Mind of Primitive Man by Franz Boas	金沢大学
	STAGE-2	06	Cognitive and language development in children	神戸大学
		07	The articulate person : a guide to everyday public speaking	お茶の水女子大学
		08	Topical Antimicrobial Testing and Evaluation	早稲田大学
		09	Spirit of the Home : How to Make Your Home a Sanctuary	大阪府立大学
		10	10 Steps to Raising a Multilingual Child	名古屋外国語大学
	STAGE-3	11	Falsifiability	広島大学
		12	New Mexico through Its Maps	静岡県立大学
		13	Advanced Reading Expert Level 2	順天堂大学
		14	The Body in Pain : The Making and Unmaking of the World	慶應義塾大学
		15	The Death of Authentic Primitive Art	静岡県立大学
	STAGE-4	16	The Righteous Mind : Why Good People Are Divided by Politics and Religion	京都大学
		17	A Calculating Mind	広島大学
		18	The Shallows : What the Internet Is Doing to Our Brains	奈良県立医科大学
		19	The Story of English	島根大学
		20	DNA Reveals That Stone Age Farmers Bred With Hunters (AFP)	上智大学

※本書に掲載している英文は、大学入試問題を使用し、必要に応じて一部改変しています。設問は新規制作しています。

大学受験　PREMIUM問題集シリーズ
英語長文PREMIUM問題集 Standard

発行日：2016年　3月30日　初版発行
　　　　2021年　9月17日　第8版発行

総合監修：**安河内哲也**
発行者：**永瀬昭幸**
　編者：東進ハイスクール・東進衛星予備校

編集担当：八重樫清隆
　発行所：株式会社ナガセ
　　　　　〒180-0003 東京都武蔵野市吉祥寺南町1-29-2
　　　　　出版事業部（東進ブックス）
　　　　　TEL：0422-70-7456 ／ FAX：0422-70-7457
　　　　　URL：http://www.toshin.com/books（東進WEB書店）
　　　　　※本書を含む東進ブックスの最新情報は東進WEB書店をご覧ください。

設問作成・英文校正：㈱CPI Japan（Craig Brantley）
　扉絵（細密線画）：丸子博史
　　　　　　　装丁：東進ブックス編集部
　　組版・印刷・製本：シナノ印刷㈱

※落丁・乱丁本は着払いにて小社出版事業部宛にお送りください。新本におとりかえいたします。但し、古書店等で本書を入手されている場合は、おとりかえできません。なお、赤シート・しおり等のおとりかえはご容赦ください。
※本書を無断で複写・複製・転載することを禁じます。

© NAGASE BROTHERS INC. 2016
Printed in Japan
ISBN978-4-89085-675-6 C7382

編集部より

この本を読み終えた君に
オススメの3冊！

英語長文レベル別問題集 ④中級編

本書「PREMIUM問題集」と同じレベル・コンセプトの『英語長文レベル別問題集』④・⑤・⑥。両方やればさらにリーディング力アップ！

一億人の英文法

日本人が英語を「話す」ための英文法書。英語の「システム」と「ネイティブの意識」を詳しく解説。スピーキング・ライティング力の向上に。

TOEIC L&Rテスト レベル別問題集 470点突破

大学生・社会人になったら必須となる「TOEIC」をレベル別にトレーニング。大学入試なんて「通過点」という意識の高い皆さんにオススメ。

体験授業

東進実力講師陣の授業を受けてみませんか？

東進では有名実力講師陣の授業を無料で体験できる『体験授業』を行っています。「わかる」授業、「完璧に」理解できるシステム、そして最後まで「頑張れる」雰囲気を実際に体験してください。

※1講座(90分×1回)を受講できます。
※お電話でご予約ください。
連絡先は付録7ページをご覧ください。
※お友達同士でも受講できます。

安河内哲也先生の主な担当講座　※2021年度
「有名大突破！戦略英語解法」「Top Level English」など

東進の合格の秘訣が次ページに

合格の秘訣1 全国屈指の実力講師陣

東進の実力講師陣
数多くのベストセラー参考書を執筆!!

東進ハイスクール・東進衛星予備校では、そうそうたる講師陣が君を熱く指導する！

本気で実力をつけたいと思うなら、やはり根本から理解させてくれる一流講師の授業を受けることが大切です。東進の講師は、日本全国から選りすぐられた大学受験のプロフェッショナル。何万人もの受験生を志望校合格へ導いてきたエキスパート達です。

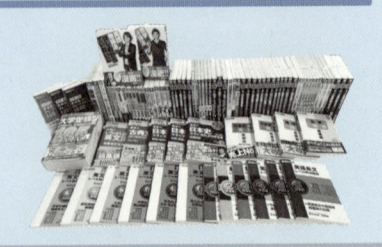

英語

安河内 哲也 先生 [英語]
日本を代表する英語の伝道師。ベストセラーも多数。

今井 宏 先生 [英語] 
予備校界のカリスマ。抱腹絶倒の名講義を見逃すな。

渡辺 勝彦 先生 [英語] 
「スーパー速読法」で難解な長文問題の速読即解を可能にする「予備校界の達人」！

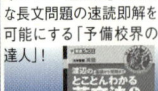

宮崎 尊 先生 [英語] 
雑誌『TIME』やベストセラーの翻訳も手掛け、英語界でその名を馳せる実力講師。

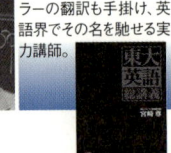

大岩 秀樹 先生 [英語] 
情熱あふれる授業で、知らず知らずのうちに英語が得意教科に！

武藤 一也 先生 [英語] 
国際的な英語資格(CELTA)に、全世界の上位5%(Pass A)で合格した世界基準の英語講師。

数学

志田 晶 先生 [数学] 
数学を本質から理解できる本格派講義の完成度は群を抜く。

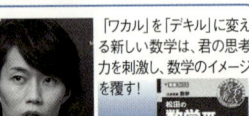

松田 聡平 先生 [数学] 
「ワカル」を「デキル」に変える新しい数学は、君の思考力を刺激し、数学のイメージを覆す！

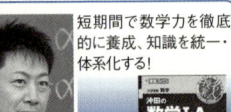

沖田 一希 先生 [数学] 
短期間で数学力を徹底的に養成、知識を統一・体系化する！

付録 1

WEBで体験

東進ドットコムで授業を体験できます！
実力講師陣の詳しい紹介や、各教科の学習アドバイスも読めます。
www.toshin.com/teacher/

国語

栗原 隆 先生 [古文]
東大・難関大志望者から絶大なる信頼を得る本質の指導を追究。

富井 健二 先生 [古文] 
ビジュアル解説で古文を簡単明快に解き明かす実力講師。

三羽 邦美 先生 [古文・漢文] 
縦横無尽な知識に裏打ちされた立体的な授業に、グングン引き込まれる！

寺師 貴憲 先生 [漢文] 
幅広い教養と明解な具体例を駆使した緩急自在の講義。漢文が身近になる！

石関 直子 先生 [小論文] 
文章で自分を表現できれば、受験も人生も成功できますよ。「笑顔と努力」で合格を！

理科

宮内 舞子 先生 [物理]
丁寧で色彩豊かな板書と詳しい講義で生徒を惹きつける。

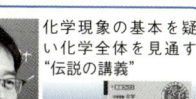

鎌田 真彰 先生 [化学]
化学現象の基本を疑い化学全体を見通す"伝説の講義"

田部 眞哉 先生 [生物]
全国の受験生が絶賛するその授業は、わかりやすさそのもの！

地歴公民

金谷 俊一郎 先生 [日本史]
入試頻出事項に的を絞った「表解板書」は圧倒的な信頼を得る。

井之上 勇 先生 [日本史]
つねに生徒と同じ目線に立って、入試問題に対する的確な思考法を教えてくれる。

荒巻 豊志 先生 [世界史] 
"受験世界史に荒巻あり"といわれる超実力人気講師。

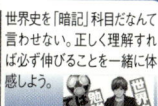

加藤 和樹 先生 [世界史] 
世界史を「暗記」科目だなんて言わせない。正しく理解すれば必ず伸びることを一緒に体感しよう。

山岡 信幸 先生 [地理]
わかりやすい図解と統計の説明に定評。

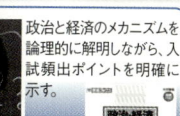

清水 雅博 先生 [公民]
政治と経済のメカニズムを論理的に解明しながら、入試頻出ポイントを明確に示す。

付録 2

合格の秘訣 2 革新的な学習システム

東進には、第一志望合格に必要なすべての要素を満たし、抜群の合格実績を生み出す学習システムがあります。

映像による授業を駆使した最先端の勉強法
高速学習

一人ひとりのレベル・目標にぴったりの授業

東進はすべての授業を映像化しています。その数およそ1万種類。これらの授業を個別に受講できるので、一人ひとりのレベル・目標に合った学習が可能です。1.5倍速受講ができるほか自宅のパソコンからも受講できるので、今までにない効率的な学習が実現します。

現役合格者の声
東京大学 理科一類
佐藤 洋太くん
東京都立 三田高校卒

東進の映像による授業は1.5倍速で再生できるため効率がよく、自分のペースで学習を進めることができました。また、自宅で授業が受けられるなど、東進のシステムはとても相性が良かったです。

1年分の授業を最短2週間から1カ月で受講

従来の予備校は、毎週1回の授業。一方、東進の高速学習なら毎日受講することができます。だから、1年分の授業も最短2週間から1カ月程度で修了可能。先取り学習や苦手科目の克服、勉強と部活との両立も実現できます。

先取りカリキュラム（数学の例）

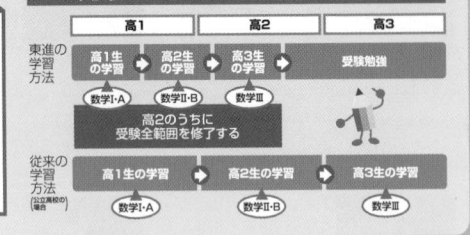

	高1	高2	高3
東進の学習方法	高1生の学習 → 数学Ⅰ・A	高2生の学習 → 数学Ⅱ・B	高3生の学習 → 数学Ⅲ	受験勉強

高2のうちに受験全範囲を修了する

	高1	高2	高3
従来の学習方法（公立高校の場合）	高1生の学習 → 数学Ⅰ・A	高2生の学習 → 数学Ⅱ・B	高3生の学習 → 数学Ⅲ

目標まで一歩ずつ確実に
スモールステップ・パーフェクトマスター

自分にぴったりのレベルから学べる 習ったことを確実に身につける

高校入門から超東大までの12段階から自分に合ったレベルを選ぶことが可能です。「簡単すぎる」「難しすぎる」といったことがなく、志望校へ最短距離で進みます。授業後すぐに確認テストを行い内容が身についたかを確認し、合格したら次の授業に進むので、わからない部分を残すことはありません。短期集中で徹底理解をくり返し、学力を高めます。

現役合格者の声
慶應義塾大学 法学部
赤井 英美さん
神奈川県 私立 山手学院高校卒

高1の4月に東進に入学しました。自分に必要な教科や苦手な教科を満遍なく学習できる環境がとても良かったです。授業の後にある「確認テスト」は内容が洗練されていて、自分で勉強するよりも、効率よく復習できました。

パーフェクトマスターのしくみ

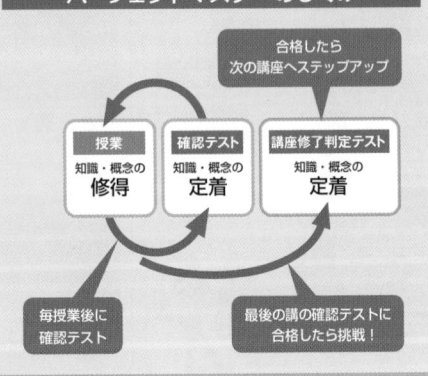

授業（知識・概念の修得）→ 確認テスト（知識・概念の定着）→ 講座修了判定テスト（知識・概念の定着）→ 合格したら次の講座へステップアップ

毎授業後に確認テスト

最後の講の確認テストに合格したら挑戦！

付録 3

東進ハイスクール **在宅受講コースへ**

東進で勉強したいが、近くに校舎がない君は…

「遠くて東進の校舎に通えない……」。そんな君も大丈夫！ 在宅受講コースなら自宅のパソコンを使って勉強できます。ご希望の方には、在宅受講コースのパンフレットをお送りいたします。お電話にてご連絡ください。学習・進路相談も随時可能です。 **0120-531-104**

徹底的に学力の土台を固める

高速マスター基礎力養成講座

高速マスター基礎力養成講座は「知識」と「トレーニング」の両面から、効率的に短期間で基礎学力を徹底的に身につけるための講座です。英単語をはじめとして、数学や国語の基礎項目も効率よく学習できます。インターネットを介してオンラインで利用できるため、校舎だけでなく、自宅のパソコンやスマートフォンアプリで学習することも可能です。

現役合格者の声

早稲田大学 政治経済学部
小林 隼人くん
埼玉県立 所沢北高校卒

受験では英語がポイントとなることが多いと思います。英語が不安な人には「高速マスター基礎力養成講座」がぴったりです。頻出の英単語や英熟語をスキマ時間などを使って手軽に固めることができました。

東進公式スマートフォンアプリ
東進式マスター登場！
(英単語／英熟語／英文法／基本例文)

スマートフォンアプリでスキマ時間も徹底活用！

1) スモールステップ・パーフェクトマスター！
頻出度(重要度)の高い英単語から始め、1つのSTEP (計100語)を完全修得すると次のSTAGEに進めるようになります。

2) 自分の英単語力が一目でわかる！
トップ画面に「修得語数・修得率」をメーター表示。自分が今何語修得しているのか、どこを優先的に学習すべきなのか一目でわかります。

3)「覚えていない単語」だけを集中攻略できる！
未修得の単語、または「My単語(自分でチェック登録した単語)」だけをテストする出題設定が可能です。
すでに覚えている単語を何度も学習するような無駄を省き、効率良く単語力を高めることができます。

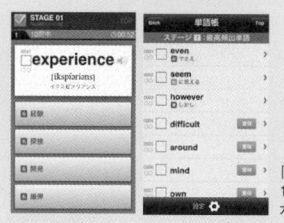

「共通テスト対応英単語1800」2021年共通テストカバー率99.8％！

君の合格力を徹底的に高める

志望校対策

第一志望校突破のために、志望校対策にどこよりもこだわり、合格力を徹底的に極める質・量ともに抜群の学習システムを提供します。従来からの「過去問演習講座」に加え、AIを活用した「志望校別単元ジャンル演習講座」が開講。東進が持つ大学受験に関するビッグデータをもとに、個別対応の演習プログラムを実現しました。限られた時間の中で、君の得点力を最大化します。

現役合格者の声

山形大学 医学部医学科
二宮 佐和さん
愛媛県 私立 済美平成中等教育学校卒

東進の「過去問演習講座」は非常に役に立ちました。夏のうちに二次試験の過去問を10年分解くことで、今の自分と最終目標までの距離を正確に把握することができました。大学別の対策が充実しているのが良かったです。

大学受験に必須の演習
■過去問演習講座
1. 最大10年分の徹底演習
2. 厳正な採点、添削指導
3. 5日以内のスピード返却
4. 再添削指導で着実に得点力強化
5. 実力講師陣による解説授業

東進×AIでかつてない志望校対策
■志望校別単元ジャンル演習講座
過去問演習講座の実施状況や、東進模試の結果など、東進で活用したすべての学習履歴をAIが総合的に分析。学習の優先順位をつけ、志望校別に「必勝必達演習セット」として十分な演習問題を提供します。問題は東進が分析した、大学入試問題の膨大なデータベースから提供されます。苦手を克服し、一人ひとりに適切な志望校対策を実現する日本初の学習システムです。

志望校合格に向けた最後の切り札
■第一志望校対策演習講座
第一志望校の総合演習に特化し、大学が求める解答力を身につけていきます。対応大学は校舎にお問い合わせください。

付録 4

合格の秘訣3 東進模試

申込受付中
※お問い合わせ先は付録7ページをご覧ください。

学力を伸ばす模試

■ 本番を想定した「厳正実施」
統一実施日の「厳正実施」で、実際の入試と同じレベル・形式・試験範囲の「本番レベル」模試。相対評価に加え、絶対評価で学力の伸びを具体的な点数で把握できます。

■ 12大学のべ31回の「大学別模試」の実施
予備校界随一のラインアップで志望校に特化した"学力の精密検査"として活用できます(同日体験受験を含む)。

■ 単元・ジャンル別の学力分析
対策すべき単元・ジャンルを一覧で明示。学習の優先順位がつけられます。

■ 中5日で成績表返却
WEBでは最短中3日で成績を確認できます。
※マーク型の模試のみ

■ 合格指導解説授業
模試受験後に合格指導解説授業を実施。重要ポイントが手に取るようにわかります。

東進模試 ラインアップ 2021年度

模試名	対象	回数
共通テスト本番レベル模試	受験生／高2生／高1生 ※高1は難関大志望者	年4回
高校レベル記述模試	高2生／高1生	年2回
全国統一高校生テスト ●問題は学年別	高3生／高2生／高1生	年2回
全国統一中学生テスト ●問題は学年別	中3生／中2生／中1生	年2回
早慶上理・難関国公立大模試	受験生	年5回
全国有名国公私大模試	受験生	年5回
東大本番レベル模試	受験生	年2回
京大本番レベル模試	受験生	年4回
北大本番レベル模試	受験生	年2回
東北大本番レベル模試	受験生	年2回
名大本番レベル模試	受験生	年3回
阪大本番レベル模試	受験生	年3回
九大本番レベル模試	受験生	年3回
東工大本番レベル模試	受験生	年2回
一橋大本番レベル模試	受験生	年2回
千葉大本番レベル模試	受験生	年1回
神戸大本番レベル模試	受験生	年1回
広島大本番レベル模試	受験生	年1回
大学合格基礎力判定テスト	受験生／高2生／高1生	年4回
共通テスト同日体験受験	高2生／高1生	年1回
東大入試同日体験受験	高2生／高1生 ※高1は意欲ある東大志望者	年1回
東北大入試同日体験受験	高2生／高1生 ※高1は意欲ある東北大志望者	年1回
名大入試同日体験受験	高2生／高1生 ※高1は意欲ある名大志望者	年1回
医学部82大学判定テスト	受験生	年2回
中学学力判定テスト	中2生／中1生	年4回

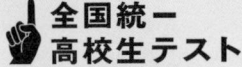

※ 早慶上理・難関国公立大模試／全国有名国公私大模試は、共通テスト本番レベル模試との総合評価。
※ 千葉大/神戸大/広島大本番レベル模試は、共通テスト本番レベル模試との総合評価。
※ 最終回が共通テスト後の受験となる模試は、共通テスト自己採点との総合評価となります。
※ 2021年度に実施予定の模試は、今後の状況により変更する場合があります。最新の情報はホームページでご確認ください。

付録 5

2021年東進生大勝利！
東大・難関大 現役合格 史上最高！ 続出

東大 現役合格 日本一！※1
816名 昨対+14名

- 文科一類 131名
- 文科二類 111名
- 文科三類 96名
- 理科一類 294名
- 理科二類 121名
- 理科三類 40名
- 推薦 23名

現役合格者の36.4%が東進生！※2
東進生現役占有率 36.4%

東進史上最高記録を更新!!
'16 742 / '17 753 / '18 725 / '19 801 / '20 802 / '21 816名

※1 東大現役合格実績をホームページ・パンフレット・チラシ等で公表している予備校の中で最多（2020年東進調べ）
※2 今年の東大全体の現役合格者は2,236名。東進の現役合格者は816名。東進生の占有率は36.4%。現役合格者の2.8人に1人が東進生です。

国公立 医・医
920名 昨対+143名
現役合格者の30.1%が東進生！
東進生現役占有率 30.1%
'19 754 / '20 777 / '21 920名
※ 今年の全大学の合格者数はまだ公表されていないため、仮に昨年の現役合格者（推計）を分母として東進生占有率を算出すると、東進生における今年の占有率30.1%。国公立医学部医学科の3.4人に1人が東進生となります。

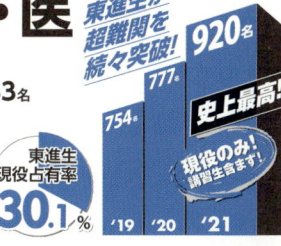

早慶
5,193名 昨対+557名 史上最高！
- 早稲田大 3,201名
- 慶應義塾大 1,992名 2年連続
'19 4,531 / '20 4,636 / '21 5,193

上理明青立法中
18,684名 昨対+2,813名 史上最高！
- 上智大 1,314名
- 東京理科大 2,441名
- 明治大 4,555名
- 青山学院大 1,943名
- 立教大 2,464名
- 法政大 3,170名
- 中央大 2,797名
'19 14,815 / '20 15,871 / '21 18,684

関関同立
11,801名 昨対+934名 史上最高！
- 関西学院大 2,039名
- 関西大 2,733名
- 同志社大 2,779名
- 立命館大 4,250名
'19 9,969 / '20 10,867 / '21 11,801

私立 医・医
671名 昨対+73名 史上最高！
'19 536 / '20 598 / '21 671

全国公立大
16,434名 昨対+598名 史上最高！
'19 14,878 / '20 15,836 / '21 16,434

日東駒専 9,094名 史上最高！ 昨対+1,094名
産近甲龍 5,717名 史上最高！ 昨対+442名

旧七帝大+東工大・一橋大
3,868名 昨対+260名 史上最高！

- **京都大** 461名 昨対+10名 史上最高！ '19 390 / '20 451 / '21 461
- **北海道大** 396名 昨対+29名 史上最高！ '19 325 / '20 367 / '21 396
- **東北大** 327名 昨対+32名 史上最高！ '19 274 / '20 295 / '21 327
- **名古屋大** 381名 昨対±0名 史上最高タイ！ '19 324 / '20 381 / '21 381
- **大阪大** 644名 昨対+104名 史上最高！ '19 524 / '20 540 / '21 644
- **九州大** 476名 昨対+34名 史上最高！ '19 370 / '20 442 / '21 476
- **東京工業大** 174名 昨対-3名 '19 160 / '20 177 / '21 174
- **一橋大** 193名 昨対+40名 史上最高！ '19 136 / '20 153 / '21 193

現役のみ！講習生含まず！

ウェブサイトでもっと詳しく
東進 [検索]

2021年3月31日締切　付録6

各大学の合格実績は、東進ネットワーク（東進ハイスクール、東進衛星予備校、早稲田塾）の現役生のみ、高3時在籍のみの合同実績です。一人で複数合格した場合は、それぞれの合格者数に計上しています。

東進へのお問い合わせ・資料請求は
東進ドットコム www.toshin.com
もしくは下記のフリーコールへ！

東進ハイスクール
ハッキリ言って合格実績が自慢です！ 大学受験なら、

0120-104-555 (トーシン ゴーゴーゴー)

●東京都

[中央地区]
- 市ヶ谷校 0120-104-205
- 新宿エルタワー校 0120-104-121
- ＊新宿校大学受験本科 0120-104-020
- 高田馬場校 0120-104-770
- 人形町校 0120-104-075

[城北地区]
- 赤羽校 0120-104-293
- 本郷三丁目校 0120-104-068
- 茗荷谷校 0120-738-104

[城東地区]
- 綾瀬校 0120-104-762
- 金町校 0120-452-104
- 亀戸校 0120-104-889
- ★北千住校 0120-693-104
- 錦糸町校 0120-104-249
- 豊洲校 0120-104-282
- 西新井校 0120-266-104
- 西葛西校 0120-104-289
- 船堀校 0120-104-201
- 門前仲町校 0120-104-016

[城西地区]
- 池袋校 0120-104-062
- 大泉学園校 0120-104-862
- 荻窪校 0120-687-104
- 高円寺校 0120-104-627
- 石神井校 0120-104-159
- 巣鴨校 0120-104-780
- 成増校 0120-028-104
- 練馬校 0120-104-643

[城南地区]
- 大井町校 0120-575-104
- 蒲田校 0120-265-104
- 五反田校 0120-672-104
- 三軒茶屋校 0120-104-739
- 渋谷駅西口校 0120-389-104
- 下北沢校 0120-104-672
- 自由が丘校 0120-964-104
- 成城学園前駅校 0120-104-616
- 千歳烏山校 0120-104-331
- 千歳船橋校 0120-104-825
- 都立大学駅前校 0120-275-104
- 中目黒校 0120-104-261
- 二子玉川校 0120-104-959

[東京都下]
- 吉祥寺校 0120-104-775
- 国立校 0120-104-599
- 国分寺校 0120-622-104
- 立川駅北口校 0120-104-662
- 田無校 0120-104-272
- 調布校 0120-104-305
- 八王子校 0120-896-104
- 東久留米校 0120-565-104
- 府中校 0120-104-676
- ★町田校 0120-104-507
- 三鷹校 0120-104-149
- 武蔵小金井校 0120-480-104
- 武蔵境校 0120-104-769

●神奈川県
- 青葉台校 0120-104-947
- 厚木校 0120-104-716
- 川崎校 0120-226-104
- 湘南台東口校 0120-104-706
- 新百合ヶ丘校 0120-104-182
- センター南駅前校 0120-104-722
- たまプラーザ校 0120-104-445
- 鶴見校 0120-876-104
- 登戸校 0120-104-157
- 平塚校 0120-104-742
- 藤沢校 0120-104-549
- 武蔵小杉校 0120-165-104
- ★横浜校 0120-104-473

●埼玉県
- 浦和校 0120-104-561
- 大宮校 0120-104-858
- 春日部校 0120-104-508
- 川口校 0120-917-104
- 川越校 0120-104-538
- 小手指校 0120-104-759
- 志木校 0120-104-202
- せんげん台校 0120-104-388
- 草加校 0120-104-690
- 所沢校 0120-104-594
- ★南浦和校 0120-104-573
- 与野校 0120-104-755

●千葉県
- 我孫子校 0120-104-253
- 市川駅前校 0120-104-381
- 稲毛海岸校 0120-104-575
- 海浜幕張校 0120-104-926
- ★柏校 0120-104-353
- 北習志野校 0120-344-104
- 新浦安校 0120-556-104
- 新松戸校 0120-104-354
- 千葉校 0120-104-564
- ★津田沼校 0120-104-724
- 成田駅前校 0120-104-346
- 船橋校 0120-104-514
- 松戸校 0120-104-257
- 南柏校 0120-104-439
- 八千代台校 0120-104-863

●茨城県
- つくば校 0120-403-104
- 取手校 0120-104-328

●静岡県
- ★静岡校 0120-104-585

●長野県
- 長野校 0120-104-586

●奈良県
- ★奈良校 0120-104-597

★は高卒本科(高卒生)設置校
＊は高卒生専用校舎
※変更の可能性があります。最新情報はウェブサイトで確認できます。

東進衛星予備校
全国約1,000校、10万人の高校生が通う、

0120-104-531 (トーシン ゴーサイン)

東進ドットコム
ここでしか見られない受験と教育の最新情報が満載！

www.toshin.com

大学案内
最新の入試に対応した大学情報をまとめて掲載。偏差値ランキングもこちらから！

大学入試過去問データベース
君が目指す大学の過去問を素早く検索できる！2021年入試の過去問も閲覧可能！
大学入試問題 過去問データベース 185大学 最大27年分を無料で閲覧！

東進TV
東進のYouTube公式チャンネル「東進TV」。日本全国の学生レポーターがお送りする大学・学部紹介は必見！

東進WEB書店
ベストセラー参考書から、夢膨らむ人生の参考書まで、君の学びをバックアップ！

付録 7

※2021年4月現在